MW00655152

The Regal Pair

DR. C.R. OLIVER

© 2004 C.R. Oliver

ISBN 1-931898-06-5

Zadok Publications Inc.
Subsidiary of OEA Intl.
P.O. Box 971
MONTGOMERY, TEXAS 77356
www.zadokpublications.com
Email: zadokbookstore@yahoo.com

Printed In United States of America

Dedication

This book is dedicated to the memory of my brother, Edmond Lee Oliver (1925-2003), Virgil McGowen, an intercessor and friend, and longtime minister and brother in Christ, Frank C. Sisson (d. 2002).

A co-dedication is to those spoken of in the book of Jude as "Dignitaries." In Jude 8, the author declared that in the last days Dignitaries will be "evil spoken of," primarily by those who have "crept in unawares." These Dignitaries are those so designated by God and His recommendation. Those who occupy this designation offer an example of Holiness and Righteousness perfection termed "glorious." They are the "glorious ones" who embrace The Regal Pair. They are present and on earth, for these are those days. Their lot bear no indignities on these pages.

Preface

Holiness and Righteousness is a subject which cuts through the morass created by the modern church. It yields its pristine features only to those willing to bow before the presence of God, Jehovah, the Almighty and reigning Son, Jesus. The Regal Pair (H&R) reign, not separately, but as a unit of glory unknown in current circles. However, to those who will become the Bride of Christ, their enthronement is welcome. The Father has always intended that those of the last days embrace this duo with a passion. Their work will bring perfection and yield a countenance as defining as Daniel's and his companions when compared to the world's fare.

As a book, The Regal Pair, offers a curative elixir for those vexed and weary of religion's failed promises. H&R is different from the fare of fools, for too long the church has "put up with fools gladly (2Corinthians 11:19)." This book's foundation is an intense study of Scripture in three dimensions: first, establishing God's definition of holiness and righteousness through His Word; second, creating an understanding about the two elements and their inseparable character and labor; third, a joyous revelation about their unique glory when viewed separately. It is in this venue the author separates the inseparable, according to grammatical and word study lines. Grammatically, they are viewed first as Holiness and Righteousness, the noun form; then as Holy and Righteous, the verb form. As Word studies, their jewel-like qualities are examined in both Old and New Testament settings.

A reader should be aware that comparisons are made in these pages which will not be found in others. Reaching back through hundreds of years, sages of past centuries reveal an understanding of the subject which has somehow been lost through time. The voices of Finney, Spurgeon and Frelinghusen speak powerfully to the current age.

One cogent truth links each of the chapters, though their arrangement may seem awkward at first. That link is the "simplicity of Christ." His Holiness and Righteousness connects with the Spirit of Holiness to bring the subject-work to life. Although H&R arrives at many doctrinal ports, like a great ship of state, its permanent home is the human heart. Their cargo is perfection, and when this ship sails into the Spirit-port of the readers mind, an awareness of spiritual refreshing will take place. In the Twenty-first Century, few have considered such perfection as possible, let alone the apprehension of the Pair personally. It is in this realm that the book is explosive, revealing "the ministry of righteousness" as body-ministry.

May those who read this material recognize that "Holy and Righteous" describes the heart of the Father and must characterize the heart of His Sons and Daughters.

Dr. Cosby R. Oliver, 2004

Contents

Chapter One: Irresistible Righteousness, Pages 1-12
Russia, A Voice from the Grave. Righteous Reckoning.
Righteousness personified.Righteousness Judges. The
Rise of Righteousness and Holiness, The Regal Pair.
A Modern Leviathan. The Spirit's Countermovement.

Chapter Two: Separating the Inseparable, Pages 13-27
Focusing on Holiness, a matter of definition. A Study of
Relational-holiness. Kingdom definitions of major theo-
logical themes is based on holiness. The home turf of
Holiness. Perfecting Holiness. Establishing Holiness.

Melbourne. The scriptures relating to character of and promises to the righteous. The testing by God. Commands to the righteous. The righteous requirement. Reaction to the righteous. Unique lifestyle of the righteous. Righteous needed on the earth. Reward of the righteous.

CHAPTER ONE

Irresistible Righteousness

Listen to Me, you who know righteousness,
You people in whose heart is My law:
Do not fear the reproach of men
Isaiah 51:7 NKJV

Those who work in foreign lands understand more than most that "righteousness has a built-in irresistible power." Missionaries enter a foreign culture and work, often times in a religious arena that has no understanding of Christ and His work; presented to them is a challenge which seems insurmountable in human terms. The Spirit of God, however, takes the missionary's example and magnifies it. People who come into contact with him or her are drawn to them supernaturally. Sometimes slowly, sometimes explosively, they find themselves ministering healing and salvation to those who cannot explain why they dismissed protocol, defied their native religion or separated themselves from family or friends. Missionaries have testified throughout centuries that somehow there is an "irresistible" element at work within them and their constituents.

History has not forgotten the lives of those who have owned holiness and righteousness. Forces were set in motion by them that continue to operate even today. The grave cannot silence their witness to the fruits of the Regal Pair (Holiness and Righteousness). Such a witness was observed in what could be termed, "A Russian's voice from the grave."

Russia, A Voice from the Grave:

Recently, an international ministry was seeking to distribute Bibles in Russia. Because of a logistics problem, the flow of Bibles from their central distribution station in Moscow slowed to a trickle and could not meet the demand for the areas they were endeavoring to cover. Being in the city of Stavropol, they heard about the history of the city in the 1930's. It was there that Stalin ordered the confiscation of all Bibles in the area. Great persecution fell upon the citizens of this city. The Christians were sent to prison, where most died. They were declared "state enemies," and their properties and belongings were taken by a vengeful police. These righteous saints underwent horrific trials for their faith.

The Bible group heard about a warehouse outside the city which had been used to house those confiscated Scriptures. They wondered if the Bibles were still there. After prayer, they requested the officials of the city to verify this as fact and allow them to use those Bibles in their activities—if their information was true. They were granted permission. The Bibles were still there.

On site, with several local laborers, the Bibles were loaded on distribution vans which would be used to reach the people of Stavropol. Among the laborers was a young student who openly declared his agnosticism, stating he was there "for the wages he would receive." During the operations, an overseer of the contract group noticed that the agnostic collegiate had disappeared. Upon searching for him, the overseer found him in a separated section of the warehouse reading one of the Bibles and weeping as he read.

Confessing his intentions to steal one of the Bibles (to sell for gain), he opened the cover to discover the name of his grandmother. Overtaken by her signature and knowing some of the persecution she had endured for her faith, he was drawn to read. Undoubtedly, she had marked sections which were her favorite passages (or written notes as many are drawn to do). Her righteousness became irresistible in that moment and drew him into the Word. God took the written Word and her testimony of righteousness and worked salvation into the heart of this unbelieving grandson. Her prayers, her faithfulness could not be daunted even by years. Righteousness, which is at the core of every holy heart, must be dealt with...its power is inherently irresistible.[1]

Generations of righteous saints have come and gone through history, seemingly passing into oblivion. They lived their lives in the Spirit, walked humbly before God, and the world judged them quaint and not noteworthy. Then, just as Jesus pronounced in Luke 11:49(NKJV), a day arrives when their righteousness must be dealt with:

> Therefore the wisdom of God also said, I will send them prophets and apostles, and some of them they will kill and persecute, that the blood of all the prophets which was shed from the foundation of the world may be required of THIS generation, from the blood of Abel to the blood of Zechariah who perished between the altar and the temple. Yes, I say to you, it shall be required of this generation.

As unfair as Jesus' message may seem, He pronounced a judgment the likes of which had never been heard in his-

3

tory. The magnitude of punishment was not understood fully by those who heard His words. Jesus said, in essence, "God and I are holding this generation responsible for ALL the blood of righteous people that has ever been shed in all of history to this point." On the surface, this pronouncement seemed ludicrous. How could this be true? Why would anyone hold one generation responsible for the actions of preceding generations? Prophetically this was similar to:

> Woe to you, Chorazin! Woe to you, Bethsaida! For if the mighty works which were done in you had been done in Tyre and Sidon, they would have repented long ago in sackcloth and ashes. But I say to you, it will be more tolerable for Tyre and Sidon in the day of judgment than for you. And you, Capernaum, who are exalted to heaven, will be brought down to Hades; for if the mighty works which were done in you had been done in Sodom, it would have remained until this day. But I say to you that it shall be more tolerable for the land of Sodom in the day of judgment than for you.
>
> Matt 11:21-24 (NKJV)

Righteousness precludes its right to judgment. Righteous judgment is always correct no matter how fierce its affront. Righteousness allowed Jesus to hold His earth-generation responsible for all the righteous blood ever shed, for they were about to shed The Most Righteous blood. But what about Chorazin and Bethsaida? Could it have been their hearts were more resistant to God than the greatest examples of polluted history? The answer is not given for this question, neither is the answer written for the judgment of the Scribes and Pharisees. The Bible only opens the reader to God-reasoning in this matter. More than just a whim of anger tempered by righ-

4

teous indignation, Jesus said His earth-generation was a judgmental turning point in history and there <u>had</u> to be a reckoning.

Righteousness carries with it a sword and a mantle. It is possessed by the heart of the Heavenly Father and dwells in like manner in every person whom the Father acknowledges. Within the scope of righteousness is the work of judgment. Judgment is built into Righteousness. Just as the Lord is righteous in His judgments, so the souls of righteous saints lead to a reckoning judgment.

Righteous Reckoning

Righteous judgment is poised in these Last Days to carry out its duties in answer to the blood of martyrs crying for their hour. THIS generation is the one upon whom the requirement falls! Prophetically this hour stands as a turning point in history, and righteous reckoning is about to take place in a way which exceeds the pronouncement about Jesus' earthly generation.

Just as Jesus required His generation to bear the judgment for all the righteous blood spilled since the beginning of time, the Twenty-first Century church is being held responsible for all the unrighteousness, the compromise, the fleshly deeds, the atrocities, the twisted doctrines and insidious hypocrisy characterizing the "church" age since the days of the Disciples.

The mantle of righteousness is falling upon those called forth to form a "kingdom of the righteous," and the "sword of righteous judgment" is about to be revealed on those not in that kingdom.

So great is this time in history that the righteous are to be known for their boldness in Him. Their holy hearts will engender spiritual deeds not recorded since the days of the prophets and patriarchs. They will be personified in the Two Witnesses slain because of their testimony but raised by God's power to walk and live again.

Undefeated, unstoppable, irresistible, the righteous are about to be revealed in power. Righteousness and holiness are inseparable in the heart of God and in the hearts of His people. Holiness and Righteousness cannot be defined apart from each other. They cannot exist apart from each other. The breath of one is the breath of the other, inseparable, because no righteousness ever existed apart from a heart made holy. (The opposite is also true; all unrighteousness in history has had its base in unholiness and unrighteousness.) Holiness seeks its counterpart in righteousness; they co-exist in the arms of each other. They are the essence of heavenly marriage and define their roles in Jesus and the Bride!

God revealed, at the offset of His earth-work (in the first five books of the Bible), that the journey into righteousness and holiness would begin within Him. He who is called "Holy" by angels and man is also known as the "righteous judge." Just as He must be reckoned with, so all Righteous souls find themselves in a world that must deal with their essence and being. Some of the world will embrace them; others will seek to destroy them, but the Righteous Man must be dealt with! Righteousness carries a sword and a mantle!

Who can deny that Jesus lived in those extremes? His righteousness exposed those who were unrighteous because the power of an endless life energized him. They wanted to kill Him. Some will want to kill the modern believer because righteousness energizes all who are His beloved.

Righteousness personified

Jesus proved this point over and again. He walked in the extremes that righteousness demands. He cleansed the Temple, yet taught the common people in the same time frame. He cleansed a temple because He responded to the outcry of righ-

6

teousness within Himself; after all, the Temple was occupied by "great pretenders." Luke 19:45 highlighted His trek of confrontation which continued to the very end of His life.

> Then He went into the temple and began to drive out those who bought and sold in it, saying to them, It is written, My house is a house of prayer, but <u>you have made it</u> a den of thieves. And He was teaching daily in the temple. But the chief priests, the scribes, and the leaders of the people sought to destroy Him, and were unable to do anything; for all the people were <u>very attentive</u> to hear Him.　　　(NKJV)

He taught the common people daily in that Temple (they were drawn irresistibly to Him), and He watched as "the pretenders" paraded. His righteousness was a constant reminder to them of their unrighteousness. During one of His teaching sessions, the chief Priest and scribes confronted His righteousness and lost their debate. Having lost, they sought to deal with the righteousness of Jesus just as pretenders do today; they sought to neutralize (the modern term for kill or publicly discredit) Him.

> So they watched Him, and sent spies who <u>pretended to be righteous</u>, that they might seize on His words...　　　Luke 20:20 (NKJV)

Yes, <u>pretense can mask being righteous</u>, but it fails when <u>it approaches its companion, holiness.</u> One may fain righteousness, but there is no way to fain holiness; this is one more reason why righteousness is covenanted with holiness.

Righteousness Judges

The same words that meant healing, salvation, and deliverance to the multitudes were the ones that exposed unrighteousness and pretense in the Scribes and Pharisees.

Jesus' righteous life gave new light to a people who were dwelling in the shadow and darkness of religious piety. Because the definition of righteousness was vague and ill-defined by hundreds of years of compromise and sin, the multitudes had grown accustomed to the vagaries of the pretenders. The pretenders ruled!

Jesus was no pretender. His life formed a genuine blend of holiness and righteousness. His righteousness poured out toward the lost and the diseased while simultaneously bringing judgment by comparison to those who lived otherwise.

Again, the "hour of the end" demands those who are righteous—to walk in that righteousness as a final call to a world grown accustomed to the pretenders. Across the universe, the righteous are about to rise to their occasion. No longer will the pretenders find smooth sailing in the "realms of the religious;" they are about to confront the "resistance of the Righteous." The sword and the mantle must be taken up by each saint, whether it causes his or her death or ends up causing revival (deep repentance and great deliverance).

Collaboration, compromise, and co-existence with the enemies of holiness and righteousness are no longer tenable. The Righteous and the Holy are separating from all who are not a part of the Regal Pair.

Centuries of silence were broken when Jesus, the epitome of holiness and righteousness, came on the scene. He held no tolerance for an institution which harbored pretenders, or those who sat in self-judgment of their own righteous standing. Just as history has its "marking points" (always before a day of beginnings), so Jesus acted as pivot between that which reeked of "the spiritually dead" and that which burst upon history "turning the world upside down."

Holiness and Righteousness transcend antiquity to confront iniquity in modern time. Jesus was thought to be Elijah, come back to earth, because His message was not based on religion's foundation, but one which was laid in eternity. The common people saw Him as the living example of the heart of God who was establishing again on the earth that which had seemingly been lost.

Religion in power (Herod, who was the prime example of religion and politics joined) quaked before Him, for he thought Jesus was John the Baptist, risen from the dead. All religion in power, whether it be Roman Catholic dominated countries or Islamic Republics, quake before true Holiness and Righteousness. Their psuedo-positions tremble before the resurrection of that which flows like a mighty river from the Holy Place of God, the true Almighty. Why? Because the righteous and holy love not their lives unto the death; they walk in a power thought dead; they face a universe of perversion and twisted morals and ethical disaster and dare call for immediate change!

John the Baptist did not fear when he spoke truth to the highest social and political figures of his day. He confronted them. The heart of Holiness and Righteousness never accommodates; it always confronts.

False religion, corrupted politics, unethical and immoral societies tremble before Holiness and Righteousness! H&R are always about a people of God joined inseparably to their God. Their presence is a living indictment—even in their silence, but let them open the wellspring of their being, and their treasures take tongue while their speech brings earthquake, thunder and fire! The religious masses had rather run for the rocks and the mountains than face their judgment because religion cowers before the Regal Pair, who expose its error and assure its demise. Such is the condemnation of Man's attempts at coalescence. Man dominated institutions crumple before these twins. They are not afraid to confront!

9

The dilemma of the Charismatic Movement has been their attempt to mold a Word of Faith movement over a body not framed in Holiness and Righteousness. The Scribes and Pharisees were living proof of the futility of such an effort. (Charismatics are not alone in this matter, for many religious organizations have toadied to the same Baal.)

Rise of Righteousness and Holiness

Ezekiel's Valley of dry bones, breathed alive by the Spirit, was a panoramic display of what is about to come upon the earth. Ezekiel's task at the Valley paled in light of establishing H&R among a people, who have had their own predetermined ideas of it. Any person who seeks to bring repentance and conviction to the corporate religious structure of today must certainly empathize with the prophet. Ezekiel literally called for ancient H&R (once occupying their life) to rise and take flesh, enabling a nation who had never seen such to grasp the difference. They were an army of the Holiness and Righteousness.

A spiritual resurrection is taking place this very hour, stirring the hearts of the faithful and true to a swelling, shaking, hungering for H&R, the likes of which has not occurred in two thousand years. Thought dead, the two witnesses rise up in the very streets that exulted in their death!

Domiciles of religious inclusion seeking to bring together "like mindedness" in the Twenty-first Century are about to witness the greatest turn to righteousness and holiness since the day of Pentecost. Seeking to organize greater groupings of ministers, congregations and institutions, through arrangements based on religious foundations already in place, will resemble Biblical Leviathan, which can only be dealt with by the likes of Holiness and Righteousness.

A Modern Leviathan: The Interfaith Movement

Already in place are cooperative efforts on diverse fronts, numbering in the hundreds. Rising up from a sea of spiritual pollution, these Dragonian efforts have leaders with bludgeoned heads long since thought slain. Robed in garments of power, the most casual observer is amazed at their resiliency. Evidence reveals how developed and ready they have been to grasp even greater power. More amazing are the scores of religious leaders who are yielding to their siren song—promising "unity," "coalition," and "combined strength." Referring to themselves as "the old guard mainstreamers," they seek havoc for those whom they label "fundamentalist-extremists."

Interfaith members range from worldwide organizations of clergy, networking for greater opportunity to sell wares and programs, to a host of duplicitous groups poised to gulp the unsuspecting and weakened multitudes. Each of them hawking his or her diverse preachment, using the same message, they declare, "let us come together." Keenly looking upon this "squirming herd in mammon's mesh," is the Lord God of Hosts, full of Holiness and Righteousness. He is joined by His "Watchers."

The Spirit's Counter Movement

Where religious enterprise will fail, the Spirit will not fail. Deep draws to deep and He is drawing the saints who have "received the kingdom (Daniel 7:18)" to their deepest commitment in history—to exhibit in flesh that which dwells within the Father: Holiness and Righteousness (the inseparable twins of God).

Holiness and Righteousness, in God and His people, are irresistible, irrefutable and incapable of defeat. The fact that holiness and righteousness exist at all in the earth today is the product of every man, woman and child in history who have triumphed in it. Sheltered now at the Highest Altar, they cry, "How long O Lord?"

CHAPTER TWO

Separating The Inseparable:
An Intense Look into Holiness

The power of God unto salvation,
applied to the mind of man, sanctifies
the soul of man and makes the mind
of man like the mind of Christ.
John G. Lake

Sanctification is possessing the mind of Christ, and all
the mind of Christ.
John Wesley[1]

T he Regal Pair are inseparable in all their demeanor and
ways. Their paths intertwine because their occupations
are the same—to bring man into the person of God! Because
of the nature of this study, it will be necessary to sometimes
partition their activities in order to fully appreciate their offices on earth.

Enormous numbers of scripture are employed to grasp
just a partial understanding of the underlying facets of both
Holiness and Righteousness; therefore, it becomes efficient

to take those passages which focus on one or the other and begin with them. Chapter One laid emphasis on Righteousness; this chapter will emphasize Holiness. Integral to this study is a review of terms.

A Matter of Terms

Paul opened Romans using words and phrases like: "separated," "Son of God, with power" and "Spirit of Holiness."

> Paul, a servant of Jesus Christ, called to be an apostle, <u>separated</u> to the gospel of God.

Speaking of Jesus, he said:

> declared to be the <u>Son of God with power</u>, according to the <u>Spirit of holiness</u>...

Then, Paul revealed the pathway to Holiness:

> <u>THROUGH whom</u> (Jesus) we have received grace.   Romans 1:1,4,5 (NKJV)

Early in his obedience to heavenly direction, Paul recognized that being "separated" was more than just being "set apart" for God's use (like a vessel upon the altar), but rather being a person of Holiness like Jesus when He was on the earth. Paul did not preach a Positional theology, but a Relational theology. His was a relational Holiness.

Relational-Holiness

Paul's comprehension of this type of Holiness would cost him rank among the Jews, mistreatment by the Roman government and misunderstanding among peers and populace. He knew that his step across the line into "separated unto Holiness" was a permanent decision with permanent consequences.

So it will be for every believer who chooses relational Holiness. The kind of separation Paul sought was the kind Moses, Aaron, the prophets and Jesus owned. The incorporation of Holiness into one's being changes the way life is defined. More or less, Holiness becomes the defining element for one's choices.

> Such a High Priest was fitting for us, who is holy, harmless, undefiled, **separate** from sinners.... Hebrews 7:26 (NKJV)

Yes, "separate" is the word Paul used. Used in connection with "holy, harmless and undefiled," its connotation is worlds apart from the definition given by an ordaining council or the high church meaning, even the symbolized meaning. It is an Old Testament meaning drawn from its roots in holiness and pictures "standing before God." Standing before God is a greater accountability than man's rationale for being separate.

Although the Epistle to the Romans harbors some of the greatest treatment and teaching in the New Testament about "righteousness," Paul rapidly established righteousness roots in holiness.

> ...now present your members to serve righteousness <u>unto</u> holiness
> ...But now freed from sin and made servants to God, ye have as your fruit (holiness) sanctification and as the end, everlasting life.
> ...the grace of God is eternal life in Christ Jesus our Lord.
> Romans 6:19,22,23b (Jubilee Bible)

By reading these verses in new light, a sequential chain emerges. <u>Looking from the external, one's service to righteousness leads to holiness. The end result is two-fold: sanctification and eternal life.</u> Thousands who can exhibit years of faithful service to ministries worldwide do not comprehend this pattern.

Paul knew there could be no service of righteousness apart

from the first born twin, holiness. Doctrines of sanctification stand meaningless without Holiness. H&R has no relevancy apart from the person of the Lord, <u>owning</u> them. One of the greatest indictments from Jesus' ministry is found in this passage:

> Also He spoke this parable to some who trusted in themselves that they were righteous, and despised others: Luke 18:9 (NKJV)

Jesus knew religious leadership had redefined the word "righteous," separating it from the root of holiness. The church has masterfully redefined sanctification, righteousness and spiritual call, separating them from their foundation of holiness and righteousness. Is it any wonder that religion flounders in a sea of mediocrity while missing God's greatest blessings?

Kingdom Definitions

The "gospel of the kingdom" dictionary, laid out by the apostles and prophets, Jesus Christ being the chief cornerstone for all ages, did not miss it! Righteousness and Holiness were connected to their every act, deed or word. They could not imagine a doctrine of salvation without holiness, or a concept of justification without holiness, or establishing a fellowship without holiness and righteousness. They could scroll down the most common church terms and phrases and gladly scribble the word, "not without holiness."

Those who labor over the "doctrine of sanctification" can now rest! There is no sanctification without holiness. Its root word is "holy," and its application is "holiness." Being sanctified means "being holy."

Thousands of sermons and millions of adjurations from seminaries to sacred halls lay emphasis on living the "separated life," but veer heartily away from the basis of that separation being "holiness." One's central being must be judged

16

"Holiness" by the "Spirit of Holiness." Many churchmen are anxious for a baptism, for a tongue, for a word, for a prophesy, but few line up for a treatment in holiness!

Paul's choice of words had Old Testament derivatives; His book-covers for Corinthians, Ephesians, Galatians should have read, "Be YE holy as I am Holy." Paul knew the people of God must have holiness as their root or their fruit would not be from God. His post Pentecost letters would be for all generations, even today's.

The "last days" generation (birthed by the Twenty-first Century) prides itself as the one to usher in Christ and the millennium, but His kingdom will not be ushered in without Holiness from the Spirit of Holiness. Holiness and righteousness will be the character of His people whose Last Day's duties come without the luxury of continued procrastination.

Just as the newly anointed Paul was force-fed huge servings of "strong doctrine" in a short period of time, so must this generation rapidly adopt the strong doctrine of Holiness. Scripture says, however, in the last days "they shall not endure strong doctrine," which is precisely the problem. Unwilling to grow up and equally unwilling to take the responsibility of holiness—myriads meander in various states of unholiness and unrighteousness.

Home of Holiness

Paul clearly defined holiness as coming "THROUGH Jesus." Jesus walked in holiness; Paul walked in holiness; both were "holiness beings." As Jesus walked among the people of Israel (who were originally called to be separated from the nations of the world in order to be a witness for God), His walk stood as judgment upon their understanding of The Regal Pair.

Legalistic and compromised by man's teaching, those who adhered to Judaism's definition of H&R did not defer to the witness of *Holiness of Being,* presented by the Messiah. Because of this discrepancy of "being," they sought to kill Him rather than emulate Him. Unfortunately, the lolling multitudes have not changed!

Paul preached the baptism of the Holy Spirit was a baptism into Holiness. Those in the upper room, awaiting His outpouring, experienced the greatest cleansing through holiness imaginable. Without one dirty thread of sin in their lives and with hearts yearning for the fulfillment of Jesus' promise in them—they were baptized into His Holiness. Though Paul was not present in that meeting, he valiantly declared that his apostleship rested on Holiness given by the same "Spirit of Holiness." As the early apostles and disciples burst upon the new day of the Spirit with flame above and inside, they did not test the waters of society—they changed it with the power of Holiness.

This last days' generation had best stop testing the waters of society (social and political relativism) and change it through the power of Holiness!

Holiness has fire power. Cloven tongues of fire were not cleansing tongues but a holiness empowering tongue. Simon stood to testify that the healing of the lame man was not the fruit of his personal power or personal holiness.

> And when Peter saw it, he answered unto the people, Ye men of Israel, why marvel ye at this? or why look ye so earnestly on us, as though by our own power or holiness we had made this man to walk?   Acts 3:12 (KJV)

This was not modesty talking, Simon knew he owned a portion of Jesus' power and Holiness. Holiness-Being has power!

Christians who long for the return of early church manifestations, must first return to early church holiness! Those who regale in the finery of "sanctification," often recoil at the austerity of holiness. "Saved, sanctified and delivered" are phrases which roll off "spiritualized tongues" as easily as "grace, mercy, love and kindness." Modern ministerial clichés lie dead before anesthetized audiences like the teaching of the great Jewish convert (Paul) lay dead before the religious leaders of his day. The veil persists. Though many were schooled in Gamaliel's classes, where theology was glibly discussed, Paul graduated from a school of higher learning which taught him a new set of definitions. Would to God all those who occupy positions of religious power had so graduated; with changed taxonomy, their preachments would be filled with the fire of Holiness.

The writer of Romans knew from the beginning his task was to bring a God-definition of H&R back into play. He thought those closest to the terms (His Jewish brethren) would receive it with ease but found them hardened to his doctrine. Paul turned to the Gentiles and took a people who had no theological background and helped them own H&R. It was their testimony, along with his, which challenged a world of darkness and successfully carried THIS GOSPEL OF THE KINGDOM to the corners of the earth.

Every dispute Paul encountered with the Temple-ites rotated around the issue of definition. He understood GRACE not just as "unmerited favor," but "favoring which brings one into the presence and power of Holiness." When Paul called for "grace to abound," He called for all the saints (people of holiness) to be brought into MORE abounding in HOLINESS!

All the definitions of Christianity are based in holiness. Grace IS wrapped in holiness, for it emanates from the God of Holiness. Mercy IS anchored in His Righteousness. Love IS the heartbeat of holiness; Love is the product of Holiness-determination. Kindness finds its root in the same soil, the

19

growth of which will end in the recipient being drawn to holiness.

Let the church return to the "dictionary of heaven" and conclude that all scripture leads to holiness, "without which no one shall see the Lord (Hebrew 12:14 NKJV)." Jesus walked in the power of Holiness, and so will His Bride!

Jesus' power was **effective** holiness. Satan took Him to the "holy" city and Jesus showed him the "City of Holiness (Matthew 4:5)." Every deed, every act, every word was a separated, sanctified, saint-filled outpouring from a Holiness Being. He lived a Holiness-determined life. To be like Jesus is to be the embodiment of Holiness!

> It is because of him that you are in Christ Jesus,
> who has become for us wisdom from God —
> that is righteousness, HOLINESS and redemption.   I Corinthians 1:30 (NKJV)

Redemption is the goal of Jesus, but it is dipped in righteousness and holiness.

There is no redemption without the Regal Pair! This is the wisdom of God!

"Is righteousness and holiness the predecessor of redemption?" Yes!

Paul knew that the wisdom that came from God was wrapped in holiness.

> Now this is our boast: Our conscience testifies that we have conducted ourselves in the world, and especially in our relations with you in the HOLINESS and sincerity that are from God. We have done not according to worldly wisdom but according to God's grace.
>   II Corinthians 13:12 (NIV)

Notice the word "grace" as it is connected to Godly wisdom and holiness. "Grace with a purpose" is grace that is

20

drawing its recipient into the Regal Pair.

Modern religionists teach a "grace" with limited purpose! Paul, however, preached "growing in grace." Grace's maturity is a Bride.

Perfecting Holiness

The Bride of Jesus must embody holiness just as the Bridegroom does—there is no other consideration, and Paul knew it when he wrote:

> Therefore come out from among them, and be ye separate, saith the Lord, and do not touch the unclean thing: and I will receive you and will be a Father unto you, and ye shall be my sons and daughters, saith the Lord Almighty. Having therefore these promises, dearly beloved, let us cleanse ourselves from all filthiness of the flesh and spirit, perfecting holiness in the fear of God.
>
> II Corinthians 6:17-7:1 (Jubilee Bible)

The universal-religious community has called God their Father and declared themselves sons with no predilection to perfecting Holiness.

Sad is the commentary, when the prophet must call those who would be "holy" to "come out" and be "separate" from the "at-large" congregation. Will the day ever come when the "at-large" congregation will repent and fall to their faces and seek holiness and righteousness above all other considerations? Although all things are possible with God, Jesus did not believe this would happen at the temple of His day, and one must draw the same conclusion today!

Ephesians, written under the same revelation as Corinthians, expressed this issue most succinctly:

> ...that ye put off everything concerning the old way of life, that is, the old man who corrupts

21

himself according to deceitful desires, and be
<u>renewed in the spirit of your understanding</u> and
that ye put on the new man, which is created
in conformity to God in **righteousness** and in
the **holiness** of truth (true holiness).

Ephesians 4:22-24 (Jubilee Bible)

Whether translated "holiness of truth" or "true holiness,"
the meaning is magnified against the lies and deceptions in
thousands of "at-large" congregations where ceremonial sanctification is pandered in place of the power of a holy life!
God's sons must be holy. God's daughters must be holy. God
is not the father of those born in illegitimacy; the DNA of His
Holiness does not course their veins, inhabit their bodies or
train their minds.

The word "saint" has its root in one word: Holy.

Man may fall and kiss the ring of one called "his holiness," but God identifies only in behalf of sons born of His
Holiness.

Our fathers disciplined us for a little while as
they thought best; but God disciplines us for
our good that we may <u>share</u> (partake) in **his
holiness**.

Hebrews 12:10 (New International Bible)

(This is one of the rare times that the NIV uses "holiness." The Spanish version uses none. The Jubilee Bible uses
"holiness" 84 times.)[2]

Whether the translators use "share" or "partake," the
meaning is the same: the believer becomes a "part" of His
holiness.

Establishing Holiness

Not only are the body of believers to exhibit holiness,
they are to be ESTABLISHED in holiness (which denotes

having a structure of holiness within the believer's frame which is recognizable and stalwart). The same word used in the passage below is used in a negative context by the New Testament, referring to established strongholds of sin that must be pulled down.

> And may the Lord make you increase and abound in love to one another and to all, just as we do to you, so that He may establish your hearts blameless in holiness before our God and Father at the coming of our Lord Jesus Christ with all His (Holiness) saints.
>
> I Thessalonians 3:12-13 (NKJV)

("Saints" are defined in Deuteronomy 33:2 as "embodied HOLINESS.")

In the establishing of hearts in holiness, a radical change must take place. No longer is self-determination to take precedence in life. Holiness-determinism is to be established!

History and the Bible report that no great move of God ever came without holiness being re-established in His people. Ezra is a prime example of re-establishing holiness as the basis for God's blessing.

Ezra 9 and 10 show not only the level of repentance required among God's people, but the drastic measures that must to be taken in order to re-establish holiness in the camp. Upon hearing the report that

> ...The people of Israel and the priests and the Levites (the people who should be holiness to God) have not separated themselves from the peoples of the lands, with respect to the abominations of the Canaanites...
>
> Ezra 9:1(NKJV)

It was Ezra who tore his garment and robe (showing contrition and that nothing personal mattered in the face of the

23

circumstances needing rectitude toward God). He plucked out some of his head and beard hair (to show symbolic contrition). The Bible says: "He sat down astonished (he had no words for such sin in the camp)." The rest of the day he sat "astonished," along with some others who feared the Lord. At the evening sacrifice, he arose from fasting (note he partook of no food until spiritual concerns were confronted), he fell on his knees and spread out his hands to the Lord his God. Note the first words he uttered all day were,

> O my God: I am too ashamed and humiliated to lift up my face to You, my God; for our iniquities have risen higher than our heads, and our guilt has grown up to the heavens...
>
> Ezra 9:6 (NKJV)

He then reviewed before the people, the mercy and grace of God as a testimony before the Lord—recounting their slavery and how God delivered them.

THEN, he voiced an immortal confession:

> 'And now, O our God, what shall we say after this? for we have forsaken Your commandments....'
>
> Ezra 9:10 (NKJV)

Then, he recounted the pitiful state of the national union: uncleanness, abomination and impurity had culminated in established relationships and marriages with those who were not holy. Seeing such gross defilement caused him to react emotionally:

> Now WHILE Ezra was praying, and WHILE he was confessing, weeping, and bowing down before the house of God, a very large congregation of men, women, and children assembled to him from Israel; for the people wept very bitterly
>
> Ezra 10:1 (NKJV)

Then, a voice from the crowd echoed the trail of sin and error and cried aloud:

> '...We have trespassed against our God, and have taken pagan wives from the people of the land; yet now there is <u>hope</u> in Israel in spite of this....'   Ezra 10:2 (NKJV)

(Note: What was the hope?)

> 'Now therefore let us make a covenant with our God to put away all these wives and those have been born to them, according to the counsel of my master and of those who tremble at the commandment of our God; and let it be done according to the law.'
> Ezra 10:3 (NKJV)

This covenant was followed by another period of mourning, and the people gathered at the house of God (in the rain) to get things right with God. Ezra again rose to a point of order,

> 'Now therefore, make confession to the Lord God of your fathers, and do His will; <u>separate</u> yourselves from the peoples of the land and from the pagan wives.'   Ezra 10:11 (NKJV)

In order to establish holiness, drastic measures had to be applied. In Ezra's day, the press toward holiness grew so strong that any area of demand was met with agreement. So drastic was this undoing and redoing, that it took months to cleanse the land and establish holiness.

(Who could imagine the heartbreak of the final moment when the man of God had to release to an unknown future—his pagan wife and children? Who could imagine the tears of misunderstanding and hours of pleading that must have traversed households occasioned by this declaration to holiness?

Who could imagine the bitter wives and crying babies that were taken back across borders and returned to their natal families? Who could imagine the longing loneliness of the day after, the emptiness and grieving that took place in the hearts of both pagan and Jew?)

Repentance is not an easy matter, nor is the establishment of holiness in land and hearth. Holiness-determinism became more important than self-determinism in every household. The blessing upon those repentant whose confessions and covenants were heard in heaven thundered as a testimony to a world not separated unto God!

It thunders a testimony to the church, the fellowships, to individuals in the Twenty-first Century! Holiness is costly, but it is an absolute with God.

How much will it take for the Twenty first Century church to establish holiness? When will the weeping astonishment begin? At what point will church leadership rip their garments ($2000 Armani suits) and bow down before the Lord and cry out, "We are too ashamed and humiliated to lift our face to You, O Lord"? At what point will the congregation begin to weep and stand at the house of God and confess their sins? At what appointed time are covenants between God and man to be honored? Name the day when the church will assemble to establish holiness in land and hearth. When will partners in liaisons be told they no longer can occupy the bed of convenience because they are not married to each other? When are children to be told the truth and repentance be manifested in their presence?

More drastic measures must be taken than "a moment of silence at a promise keepers meeting." More weeping must be done than the tertiary repentance occasioned by a sporadic, convicting sermon. More confession must come forth than can be forgiven in a confessional booth or a Christian

26

counselor's room. Somehow, somewhere, sometime, in the not too distant future, a body of believers is going have to get serious about establishing holiness—ONLY then will it begin. What begins as a sniffle could break forth into open weeping, then a confession loud enough to be heard in heaven—THEN, maybe heaven will be moved, and a covenant to establish holiness be approved. BUT UNTIL THEN, the only call from heaven is, "come ye out from among them."

CHAPTER THREE

Holiness Magnified

"Pursue Holiness, without which no one will see the Lord"
Hebrews 12:14

C.G. Finney: Personal Holiness

1850 found C.G. Finney powerfully convinced that much of what the church of his day believed and taught about salvation was in direct conflict with revealed Scripture. His messages during this time reflected the culmination of his own personal introspection regarding the subject of holiness. Much of this took place, as evidenced in his journals, in Boston, during the winter of 1843-44. In essence, he rejected any preachment of salvation that was not based on personal holiness. He magnified holiness to his audiences during this period.

(Once again, it is necessary to Magnify Holiness before the people of God. Techno-Christianity has focused on almost every aspect of the Christian experience except Holiness, which is foundational for a walk with God.)

Finney, because of personal experience, believed it necessary to keep a constant eye upon the spirit-heart.

> Persons who do not like to have their hopes
> tried, and themselves searched, do great wrong
> to their souls...the man who is seeking to be
> sanctified, desires to be searched that he may
> not be resting in any degree upon an uncertain
> and unsafe foundation.[1]

Based on this premise, Finney took to task those who sought salvation through making the gospel a vehicle of convenience.

> Many are really seeking to be justified in sin.
> They ask God to pardon them, but they refuse
> to be sanctified; they seek Christ as their jus-
> tification only. They cleave to their sins, they
> are living in their sins, and they seek to be jus-
> tified rather than sanctified—indeed, they
> refuse to be sanctified at all.[2]

Finney struggled with "unsanctified professors of religion" in his day; but alas, that group has multiplied and become the majority in religious circles in the Twenty-first Century. Silence reigns in pulpit and pew where the subject of sanctification is concerned. Morality and ethics lessons have taken the place of personal holiness from pulpit to bible study. True Holiness is not premised on Pharisaical moral and ethical duty; it is based on relationship.

Holiness-Relationship

Here are a few of the quotes from Mr. Finney's sermon:

> Men cannot be Christians unless they are
> holy...
> Multitudes make this mistake—they seek hope
> rather than holiness...
> He (the churchman) has no right to expect to

30

get to heaven unless the work of sanctifica -
tion is going on in his soul...

The individual seeks much more to be par-
doned than to be made holy...

All idea about Christ being the believer's sanctification, or that sanctification as a condition
of salvation is wholly lost sight of...

There is no stress laid upon the doctrine of
sanctification...

Whenever the doctrine of justification comes
to be more prominent in the church than sanctification, there is something wrong, there is a
radical error crept into the church....

A man who lives in any sin, any form of self-
pleasing, and self-seeking, cannot be a Christian....

Believer in Christ (addressing the audience),
the Lord hath set you apart for himself, separated you from the rest of the world; but you
are only set apart as 'holiness to the Lord:' it
must be written plainly upon you;...

You must become holy in order to become
happy....[3]

Finney's theology, when reviewed in this form, penetrates
and destroys the illusions of much faith-based teaching which
does not stress as its premise personal holiness. Holiness is
treated like righteousness, as an option, which may or may
not be a part of the Christian's life. Holiness is not an option;
it was not so to Finney; it is not so to God. Mr. Finney did not
come to these conclusions short of a personal confrontation
within his own soul.

Finney first battled with the matter of holiness within himself and settled the matter prior to his preaching the cited

messages. As indicated, in Boston, in the winter of 1843-44, his journals reflect the work of the Spirit within him (such work must take place within every person who seeks The Regal Pair). Finney soon, however, discovered that he had no preaching audience for these most personal and foundational beliefs. As the reader looks into the following excerpts, let him or her ask, "Where is the forum for such discussion today?"

> I read nothing else, all that winter, but my Bible; and a great deal of it seemed new to me...
>
> Holiness to the Lord seemed to be inscribed on all the exercises of my mind...
>
> I presume the people were more sensible than I was myself, of the great change in my manner of preaching...
>
> At this it seemed as if my soul was wedded to Christ...
>
> The language of the *Song of Solomon*, was as natural to me as my breath.
>
> Indeed the Lord lifted me so much above anything that I had experienced before, and taught me so much of the meaning of the Bible, of Christ's relations and power and willingness, that I often found myself saying to Him, 'I had not known or conceived that any such thing was true'[4]

Finney could hardly wait to share with his audience the matters of holiness that were coursing his every waking moment, but he found resistance. Here are a few excerpts from the same memoirs:

> The people of the churches generally were in no state to receive my views on sanctification;

32

and although there were individuals in nearly all the churches, who were deeply interested and greatly blessed, yet as a general thing the testimony that I bore was <u>unintelligible</u> to them....

It does seem to me infinitely important that there should be a higher standard of holiness in Boston....

These are experiences in which I have lived a great deal since that Time (speaking of 1843-44). But in preaching I have found that <u>nowhere</u> can I preach those truths on which my own soul delights to live, and be understood, except it be by a very small number....

I have found the churches in so low a state as to be utterly <u>incapable</u> of apprehending and appreciating what I regard as the most precious truths of the whole Gospel....

But as a matter of experience they are <u>ignorant of the power</u> of the highest and most precious truths of the Gospel of salvation in Christ Jesus.[5]

(A more concise evaluation of modern religion cannot be found!)

Finney discovered a few individuals interested in holiness, but judged the majority not only ignorant but "incapable" of sustained preaching on the subject. (So it is today!)

Personal experience led Finney to embrace a doctrine of sanctification which included a true knowledge of holiness and with it, a life changing belief that all Scripture is predicated on understanding and embracing holiness.

Habitation of Holiness

Today, with such great emphasis on Last Days' Theology, personal holiness has been relegated to a back row, if any row at all.

Yet, every passage in the Bible referring to the coming day of the Lord is wrapped in Holiness. Scholars may attempt to place emphasis elsewhere, but true scholarship must emphasize a holy people, living in the presence of holiness, as the foremost attribute of God's last day glorious church. Unless the modern church becomes the "court of holiness" on earth, its only course is desolation!

Holiness simply **must** come upon the earth in order to be in cadence (synchronized step) with the holiness of heaven.

The upper room in the New Testament became a "habitation of holiness" as a waiting "people of holiness" were endued with power by the "Spirit of Holiness." Afterward, they became living examples of holiness for all succeeding generations to follow. In life and in death, at the core of their Being, they lived in the flame of the Spirit of Holiness.

That flame has not diminished, nor has its power to produce holiness in the people of the Lord. Holiness is alive upon the earth, but alas—not in the majority of those claiming Christianity as their possession. A modern book of Acts will never be written by the religious sets of today. To them, holiness exists "out-there" but nowhere this side of heaven. Those who walk in the baptism of the Spirit of Holiness know holiness and heaven are nearer to earth than others imagine.

Holiness, for the early disciples, lessened the distance between earth and heaven. Alive on earth or alive in heaven—their journey was exactly the same; they lived in holiness. Holiness is not a way of life; it is life. Without Holiness, there is no prospect of heaven. For the Holiness Ones, travel from an earth walk to a heaven walk is the same walk. Through the valley of death or translation, it is a simple matter of (same Lord, same authority over life, same point of reference)— holiness. God's heaven is a habitation of Holiness.

The prophets were joined to the early disciples in their reverence for personal holiness because that is how the Lord, Himself, lives:

> ...Look down from heaven, and behold from
> the habitation of thy holiness and of thy glory....
> (Isaiah 63:15, Jubilee Bible)

Peter and his brethren's understanding of the subject stand as judgment to current theological beliefs about the nature and identity of holiness. Cajoling messages, tidbits of goodwill, sermons on success, time management and the universal brotherhood of man, seem to pale next to the "habitations of thy holiness."

Holiness Not an Option

The death on the Cross was not to engender what passes itself for Christian holiness today; it was to restore man to a true state of holiness in order to be in fellowship with the God of Holiness. Eden was once a paradise of holiness, and the price of Calvary was to bring man into the Garden of God, the kingdom of holiness. Sadly, the masses who declare their allegiance to the Lord have never been taught this. If this were not true, there would be no whining homophiles claiming to be Christian, demanding their rights. Are they unaware they march toward the prospect of Sodom? Likewise, those who salute the Interfaith message, calling for tolerance of all world religions, must consider their faith-base far removed from holiness. The Courts of His holiness belong to Him alone; none but His Holy Ones will tread them!

Currently, Holy hearts are breaking over the carnage of souls deceived and lied to on a weekly basis, as religious leadership stands to declare a different gospel than the kingdom of Holiness. Jeremiah voiced similar concern centuries ago, "My heart is broken within me because of the prophets (who bear a false message) (Jeremiah 23:9 NKJV)."

Anyone, with any compassion about him, finds his "weeper about wept out," over the condition of leadership in modern congregations. True men of God say with Jeremiah, "I was like a drunken man, and like a man whom wine has overcome, before the LORD, and before the words of his HOLINESS (Jeremiah 23:9 Jubilee Bible)." The foundation of all scripture is the "words of His Holiness." Multitudes read them as glibly as the newspaper and walk away from their reflection without repenting. David could not be so taciturn:

> Hear the voice of my supplications when I lift
> up my hands toward the oracle of thy holiness.
> Psalms 28:2 (Jubilee Bible)

Oracles of Holiness-wisdom, pouring forth to people of holiness, should be the fare of sermons and the feast of congregations. Cause to weep is furthered when one assays the condition of the masses who receive tidbits soaked in "pacifism" as substitutes for "oracles clothed in holiness."

Anesthetized on Sunday morning, the multitudes stagger into the streets of cities and villages, having received nothing of holiness, but having visited what has been wrongfully described as worship in a holy place!

Temple worshippers, in the post resurrection era of Jesus, had no comprehension of what the disciples were doing when they worshipped and praised God continually (Luke24:53). The "Templers" who stumbled through the prophets and the ministry of Jesus were being consistent with their inner man. They were consistently wrong! Today, those who seek to worship without holiness receive no better fare!

Jeremiah's first sermon and prophetic word was directed

to what should have been a holy people; but instead, they had deteriorated to the sad epitaph known as: "the nation long ago called Holy."

> Thus said the LORD: I remember thee, the mercy of thy youth, the love of thine espousals, when thou didst go after me in the wilderness, in a land that was not sown, Israel **was holiness** unto the LORD and the first fruits of his increase..
>
> Jeremiah 2:2-3a (Jubilee Bible)

The embodiment of Holiness is what the congregation of the Lord was designed to be. God remembered a time when they loved Him in holiness. Alas, the **WAS** of verse three glares in marked opposition to anyone called "HOLY!" (Could it not be said of most churches, denominations, waning spiritual movements—they are a fruitless land that once WAS holiness to the Lord?) God is not content to deal with a "has been" situation.

Jeremiah prophesied about a day to come when the liberated redeemed will say of their city,

> The LORD bless thee, O habitation of justice (righteousness) and mountain of holiness.
>
> Jeremiah 31:23 (Jubilee Bible)

Now that will be a good day, but it is not this day!

O, Church! will this day ever arrive for you? Shall the people ever embrace holiness and be able to refer to their fellowship as a dwelling of righteousness and holiness? Many shrug their shoulders and ruminate that Israel was always backsliding and repenting, backsliding and repenting, thus setting a pattern for the church. Israel, however, ran into the brick wall of 79A.D., and it took them nearly two thousand years to recover. Is it not true that the voice of the Great Prophet (Jesus) and His forerunner (John the Baptizer) gave one mes-

37

sage to this retinue? Repent, for the kingdom of heaven is at hand! (Exactly the message for the modern church!) Jesus and John had their predecessors.

Malachi accused Judah (the people of praise) of dealing treacherously and committing abomination while continuing to give offerings and weeping (feigning repentance) before the altar. "Judah has profaned the holiness of the LORD by loving and marrying the daughter of a strange god (Malachi 2:11 Jubilee Bible)." (The modern church has also married some strange gods.)

The church has profaned the holiness of the LORD by loving and marrying wealth, success and choosing political correctness over holiness! Here is where similarity ends, for now a difference is made between Ancient Israel and the modern church. Here is the difference. There are no prophets of God who would be allowed to speak the oracle of God in the modern setting. License, to speak to the unholy global mess called the church, is only granted from those who themselves are unholy. A holy prophet, a holy ministry wouldn't stand a chance for approval. This is the reason most churches are barren of holiness. Without the base of holiness, church messages on love sound like seduction, and their sermons mix with a thousand other voices to beckon to greater number of unsuspecting passersby!

A God who speaks out of His Holiness must have a people who hear out of theirs. The early Disciples uttered, "We can but speak what we have seen and heard." This was their legal right! A church has no legal voice but the voice of holiness. Holiness or hypocrite: that is the choice.

"The Lord has sworn by his holiness," is a phrase used multiple times in the Psalms. The following is a much repeated phrase, not only in the focal passage but several others.

God has spoken in His holiness...
Psalms 60:6; 89:35; 108:7)

The Lord <u>owns</u> His holiness. One cannot speak out from something that one does not own. It belongs to Him. "In His holiness," speaks of who He is inwardly. His whole Being is Holiness, and there is no other point of reference. (The Body of Christ must swear by "their holiness" or resign its creed and credential. Based on Him, built through Him, surrounded by Him, they must be Holiness to Him.)

Holiness-Determined

Every aspect of the life of the believer (private and corporate) is connected to God through Holiness. From worship to spiritual warfare, the basis of very prayer and preachment finds its core in holiness.

Boast, as many do, on the size of the worship team, or the number in the choir, or the charisma of their pastoral leader but fail in the area of holiness, and the church has no credibility with God or credential with man. The church can experience no worship aside from holiness.

David defined worship as: Holy people praising God (in the beauty of holiness), with Holy hands lifted, giving thanks and remembrance (Psalms 30:4) of His holiness. It is time for a great cry to come from every place that boasts a sanctuary affirming agreement with David's conclusions in Psalms 93:5.

Holiness becometh thy house, O Lord.
(NKJV)

This was the plan of God from the beginning, that holiness cloth His people in praise.

The song of Moses and the redeemed (Exodus 15:11) was a song of holiness.

Who is like YOU, *glorious in holiness* <u>fearful in praises</u>, doing wonders? (NKJV)

39

When Moses was given the blueprint for the tabernacle and its furnishings, holy places were to be filled with "holy" things. The High priest wore a crown with, "Holiness unto the Lord," engraved in pure gold. (Revelation's crowns sit atop twenty-four elders in the court of His Holiness, who cast their golden crowns before Him who lives forever and ever. Inscribed on those crowns is: "Holiness Unto the Lord!" Those who surround the Throne are holiness to Him.) The holy people of earth will have fellowship with the holy people of heaven.

Holiness, the basis for Christian Fellowship

When Holiness looks upon Holiness, a fellowship begins which is not like the camaraderie of the natural world. It is first holy, then it is cross-identifiable. Such fellowship is a mutuality born from the Holy One's understanding of the companionship of the holy—an understanding which runs deep into the inner being and accepts the magnitude of the deposit of God within the fellow spirit! Holiness is built upon relationship (Vertical and horizontal relationship)!

Holiness is recognizable as it resides in others. Holiness draws holiness to its bosom and delights in its charms. The fellowship of holiness **is** the fellowship of the true church. There is no other basis for communion.

Such Holiness finds its roots in God Himself and it gives the Father pleasure to preside over a people like Himself. Holiness affords more than the luxury of saying, "I am in the image of God!" It declares: "God's Holiness Image resides in me; I think as He thinks and love what He loves."

God's children are more than an Adamic image showing a genetic trail; God's children have holiness as their core or they don't have God! Holiness, then, becomes the line of demarcation (the line drawn in the sand) between the people of the world and the people of the Lord.

Holiness is the distinctive attribute common to the people of God, a quality not understandable among those in religion and the world. Ezekiel underlined this fact when he spoke of the angel having the inkhorn who came forth to mark those who were "holiness unto the Lord."

> 'Go through the midst of the city, through the midst of Jerusalem, and put a mark on the foreheads of the men who sigh and cry over all the abominations that are done within it.'
>
> Ezekiel 9:4 (NKJV)

In the last days of history, God will have a people of holiness who sigh and cry over all the abominations that are done! Many are sighing and crying already over the abominations of the church. They are in the earth now! Their presence is already being felt; their prayers are already bringing judgment!

Holiness Must be Reckoned With

Holiness, of being, demands a response from an unholy world, just as righteousness-being judges the world condition. Let holy men of God enter the scene and the scene will change (both the Old and New Testaments give ample examples of this fact). An Elijah or Elisha on today's scene would cut a swath through standard religion that would leave a trail of wailing a mile wide. Holiness on the scene demands repentance and change. (Allow a Samuel to appear and the compromised Saul's will start to blabber.)

History is moved by holy men of God. One Daniel, in the midst of a nation, changes the nation. One Holiness David, before an army, drags a bloodied head in victory. There is power in holiness. "BE (state of being) ye holy as I am holy," is a call to majesty, power and a stature of impregnability (the armor of God will not a fit an unholy frame).

41

Holiness dwells beneath the armor of righteousness, salvation, faith, truth, the preparation of the gospel, for it is the only body fit to wield the Spirit-sword. Holy people are powerful people.

Daniel 12:7 declared, in the last days, it will be the power of the Holy People which will be in the persecutor's crosshairs.

> ...that it shall be for a time, times, and a half (or three and one-half years); and when <u>they have made an end</u> of shattering and crushing the <u>power of the holy people</u>, all these things shall be finished   (Amplified Bible)

Daniel saw two men, standing on either side of the river (of time). They may well represent symbolic religious forces from the East and the West. Their interest is clearly focused upon shattering to pieces the power of the holy people.[6] (See addendum 2, *Crushing of the Holy Ones*) They inquire of the angel in authority as to when all this will happen. They are told, "at the end of time." Today, right now, the holy people of God stand in the midst of the beginning of a shattering. They are ready for the battle, though. True holy people look more like Gideon's three hundred, more like a remnant, far fewer in number than a modern reviewer wishes to comprehend (See Chapter Six).[7]

Reviewing Holy Ground

Perhaps it is time for someone to rise up and say, "The Bible is more literal than first thought; Yes, perhaps Jesus **meant** a real camel and a real needle." Yes, He meant, "narrow is the way and few their be that find it." Absolutely, it is true: "If anyone defiles the temple of God, God will destroy him. For the temple of God is <u>holy, which temple ye are. Let no one *deceive* himself </u>(I Corinthians 3:17-18a NKJV)." Without doubt, it clearly means: "without holiness, no one

42

will see the Lord (Hebrews 12:14)."

Early in the Bible, God spoke, "...if you will indeed obey My voice and keep My Covenant...you shall be to Me a king-dom of priests and a <u>holy</u> nation (Exodus 19:5,6 NKJV)." Every evidence indicates this was a covenant of holiness. Every evidence further indicates it was God's purpose to have a "people of holiness." Today, there are many attempts at priesthood without mention of the holy. Repeatedly God ham-mered a single truth to Israel:

> For I am the LORD your God. You shall there-fore sanctify yourselves, and <u>you **shall be** holy</u>: for I am holy.   Leviticus 11:44 (NKJV)

Again, He rehearsed:

> Speak to all the congregation of the children of Israel, and say to them: <u>You **shall be** holy</u>, for I the LORD your God am holy.
> Leviticus 19:2 (NKJV)

Leviticus 20:7 (NKJV) says,

> Sanctify yourselves therefore, and be <u>holy</u>, for I am the Lord your God.

Once more, Leviticus 20:26 (NKJV) says,

> And <u>you **shall be** holy</u> to Me, for I the LORD am holy, and have <u>separated you</u> from the peoples, that you should be Mine.

Today, congregations claim wondrous promises, little knowing those promises are for the holy people. Israel, in Moses' time, made a similar mistake; they surmised that "all the congregation is holy (Numbers 16:3)." Standard reason-ing by man, then, concludes, "We are holy because we are the congregation." The arrogance by which they addressed Moses betrayed their unholy hearts. (Arrogance in the modern reli-gious system Still betrays unholy hearts.) Arrogance was tan-

43

tamount to Korah's declaration to Moses. Therefore, Moses' solution is about to take place; God is about to reveal who are His and who are holy. Look Out, Ye modern Korah's, for death waits at your door.

An overlooked aspect of the Moses-Korah confrontation looms, however. Moses' actions were to be examined as would Korah's confederates—in the morning. Moses' heart was confident as the sun rose, but Korah awoke to foreboding!

Morning has broken on the last days; presumption is about to be judged. Numbers 15:30 testified against this sin of "presumption," by picturing it as the awful spectacle of attempting to stand in the place of God while trying to officiate in the affairs of God.

Congregations, boards and bodies of religion, along with their constituents, have taken too many liberties and acted in areas where God has not given them permission to preside. Assuming that "all the congregation" is a decisive unit, empowered by their corporate decision, thereby sanctioned by God, is a fatal error. It was the Lord who pointed out, in Numbers 15:39, that harlotry of heart and eye is the natural bent of rational mankind. Corporate harlotry of heart is the quintessence of presumptive reasoning, it seeks to replace God's leadership in the everyday affairs of His people.

Serious business followed the sunrise showdown. Ferreting out the unholy ones became Moses' responsibility, for both God and Moses knew un-holiness would stop the blessing of the Lord. Today, Moses is not here! Those who cry, "The congregation is holy"—have based their belief on theological error; they reveal their wanton hearts.[8] Today, instead of a Moses searching for a few of the unholy, the opposite is taking place; the unholy are seeking to eject the holy! Moses fell on his face; they dig in their heels!

Deuteronomy 7:6 (NKJV) addressed what should be the

44

true nature of all congregations:

> For you are a holy people to the LORD your
> God; the LORD your God has chosen you to
> be a people for Himself, a special treasure
> above all the peoples of the earth

No greater invective could be issued than was issued in Deuteronomy 26:19 (NKJV):

> ...He shall set you high above all nations which
> He has made, in praise, in name, and in honor,
> and that you may be a holy people to the LORD
> your God, just as He has spoken.

Psalms 24:3-5 (NKJV) reviewed with graphic sweep that which is required of the holy:

> Who may ascend into the hill of the LORD?
> Or who may stand in His holy place?
> He who has clean hands and a pure heart,
> Who has not lifted up his soul to an idol,
> Nor sworn deceitfully,
> He shall receive blessing from the LORD and
> Righteousness from the God of his salvation.

The Regal pair are once again together in these verses, and as this book progresses, their work will become synonymous with "the saints." (Deuteronomy 33:3 used the word Holiness instead of "saints.")

> And He shall come with ten thousand of His
> **holiness**   (Jubilee Bible)

According to David, holiness must first be at the core, then righteousness can come through the door.

CHAPTER FOUR

Extreme Righteousness

A scepter of righteousness is the scepter of Your kingdom.
Psalms 45:6 NKJV

Two books in the New Testament carry the most teaching about righteousness and holiness in combination; they are Romans and Hebrews. Since these books were both directed to Jewish Christians initially, it bears pointing out that the Jews were surely the most spiritually educated people on earth (at that time) regarding these two subjects. Why would Paul and the writer of Hebrews spend time addressing those schooled in Judaic principles and discipled by the apostles on the subject of the Regal Pair? Could it be that they were laying foundations for an extreme form of righteousness and holiness when compared to the accepted form of their day? Could it also be they were convinced deceit and error regarding these subjects had to be countered in clearer terms?

Righteousness that Exceeds The Pharisees

Jesus looked over the most well educated and theologically correct subsection of the established religion of His day and taught thusly:

> For I say unto you, That except your righteousness shall <u>exceed</u> the righteousness of the scribes and Pharisees, ye shall in no case enter into the kingdom of the heavens.
>
> Matthew 5:20 (Jubilee Bible)

Why did He single out these two groups for special treatment? Scribes copied and handled the Word of God on a daily basis. They revered the name of God beyond anything viewed today. They were biblical experts, often working hand in hand with the Pharisees.

The Pharisees produced the largest number of theologically sound Torah believers in their day. They tithed down to the least resource and gave themselves to fasting, praying and ceremonial purity. Their definition of righteousness extended beyond much of the Law, and they practiced meticulous adherence to the smallest of details. They believed in angels, casting out demons, healing and sacrifice. Their numbers constantly guarded against the liberalism of sectarian Sadducees. Family was important to them, as was the keeping of the ten commandments. They never failed to observe the Sabbath, to offer sacrifice for their sins, observe the feasts of Passover, Pentecost and Tabernacles. They taught their children to read and memorize the scriptures and blessed Rabbis that taught in their midst. Pharisees were as astute in business as they were in spiritual matters. They discussed issues of importance openly and often sat in the gates as judges on matters of the Law and the Prophets. Comprehension of the slightest details coursed their minds, as they memorized scripture and could quote all of the first five books of the Bible. They knew the teachings of the prophets, prided themselves in the fact they were sons and daughters of Abraham

48

and considered themselves blessed of God. David was their King of kings, and his throne was superimposed in their minds. His songs were memorized as was the music accompanying them. They danced before the Lord and gave praise and prayer. They contributed liberally to the needs of the community in alms and offerings. They cared for their brethren and walked circumspectly in the affairs of life. They condemned adultery, fornication and the sins of the flesh. They upheld the Temple and Jerusalem foremost in their mind and waited for a greater Jerusalem and a wondrous Messiah.

Modern Pharisees

If a congregation of modern dimension had just a handful of these Pharisees today, their position would not be minor, for they would be asked often to the platform and given opportunity to testify and prophesy without measure. Their gifts would be mentioned often, as would their offerings to the various causes and building programs of the church. They would be honored at banquets, featured in video shorts and ordained as elders and deacons. Their style would be emulated and projected as superior, proffered as examples of Christian living. Their entrance to gospel business men's meetings, promise keepers and various success-oriented organizations would be guaranteed. Hailed as leaders, with gifted talents, they would anoint with oil, believe for miracles and quote proper passages in scripture to affirm their faith. BUT...Jesus said without equivocation: unless one's righteousness exceeded theirs, one would not enter the kingdom of heaven. (All of the good things that could be said of the Pharisees was destroyed in light of this pronouncement.)

At the core of the Pharisee's heart was a missing ingredient, holiness. Therefore, none of his deeds were accounted for righteousness. (Let the record show that righteousness is a matter of extreme importance to God, and extreme righteousness goes beyond the wildest concepts of modern congregations.)

No doubt the reader, upon examination of the life and habits of the Pharisees, would have evaluated them high on the spiritual scale of rectitude. Jesus rated them low. What caused this disparity of value? To answer this question, it is necessary to examine righteousness first in its noun-form as it relates to "person," then move to the adjective- form used as a descriptor. Righteousness, in this chapter, will be treated much like Holiness was treated in the former chapters.

Jesus: a person of extreme righteousness

Nearly all scriptures used in prophetic uttering, about the coming of Jesus as Messiah, synonymously used righteousness as a part of His kingdom. When He arrived, righteousness became a pivotal part of His kingdom message.

> 'Behold, the days are coming,' says the LORD,
> 'That I will raise to David <u>a Branch of righteousness</u>; A King shall reign and prosper, And <u>execute judgment and righteousness</u> in the earth. In His days Judah will be saved, And Israel will dwell safely; Now this is His name by which He will be called: THE LORD OUR RIGHTEOUSNESS.'
>
> Jeremiah 23:5-6 (NKJV)

Manifest destiny required Jesus to be the "man of righteousness" He is, because the fulfillment of prophesy required it. Daniel's end time vision pictured the "man of righteousness" bringing about the closure of history.

> 'Seventy weeks are determined
> For your people and for your holy city,
> To finish the transgression,

To make an end of sins,
To make reconciliation for iniquity,
To bring in **everlasting righteousness,**
To seal up vision and prophecy,
And to anoint the Most Holy.'

Daniel 9:24 (NKJV)

Jesus practiced an **extreme form** of righteousness. It is that extreme righteousness He taught His followers and pressed upon them. Repeatedly, He warned his disciples and followers to stand out in CONTRAST to the Scribes and Pharisees. Scribes and Pharisees developed their understanding of righteousness on error. They reasoned their authority on their lineage to Abraham, while Jesus based His authority on His lineage to one greater than Abraham. Jesus embodied righteousness through faith; they did not! The righteousness that came by faith was the true Abrahamic form; the righteousness they expressed was not. Abrahamic righteousness looked for a city whose builder and maker was God, a place to dwell. It identified with the people of God and looked for a city with foundations not made by man. Righteousness expressed by the Scribes and Pharisees could never find its way to such a kingdom.

Matthew 5:20 was a life-long teaching for Jesus, not because of the problems He encountered at the hands of the Scribes and Pharisees, but because their view toward righteousness was corrupted and had to be countered. If their form was correct, then His gospel was in error. Jesus, therefore, practiced and continually taught an **extreme form** of righteousness unknown to them. The Old Testament said, "Let the wicked forsake his Way and the Unrighteous man his THOUGHTS (Isaiah 55:7, NKJV)." Isaiah also said,

Let grace be shown to the wicked, Yet he will not learn righteousness; In the land of upright-

51

ness he will deal unjustly, and will not behold
the majesty of the LORD.

Isaiah 26:10 (NKJV)

After every encounter with the Scribes and Pharisees (many of the Scribes were Scribes of and for the Pharisees), He would cleanse himself either by exposing their moves to his disciples or by moving to a desolate area to pray. Some of His greatest displays of compassion and emotion, however, followed these encounters. True righteousness does not always display itself in indignation and temple cleansing; sometimes it weeps over a people who have no other example than Scribes and Pharisees and who are mislead in their observations.

Righteousness was broader, more comprehensive, to Jesus than "those of religion." His comprehension of the scope of righteousness gave Him unlimited freedom and powerful direction. True righteousness is limitless in its expression and finds itself in every righteous act, deed and word. It has an authority based on the word of the Lord. It causes actions that must find fulfillment; its deed are those which MUST be accomplished on the earth. Righteousness speaks of person; it characterizes the inner man as does holiness. When someone exclaims, "That person is a righteous person," he or she use an adjectival descriptor for a noun form. It could easily be said like this, "That person is a person of righteousness." By doing so, the identity flows back to God—for it is said of Him, "The Lord Our Righteousness (Jeremiah 33:16)." The prophet declared also, "the Lord **lives...in righteousness** (Jeremiah 4:2)." Compared to kingdom righteousness, that form practiced by the Scribes and Pharisees became increasingly despicable. Jesus sought to make clear to His people, that to practice the form used by the Scribes and Pharisees meant death—to practice His form meant life.

Just a simple review of the scriptures relating to Scribes and Pharisees causes the examiner to garner the reason for Jesus' repeated messages. Such a study will also reveal the necessity to preach an **extreme righteousness** today. Extreme righteousness is necessary in order to teach the world-at-large the difference between a true follower of Jesus Christ and those of professional Christianity. Current theology yields a muddled view of true righteousness and leaves its student struggling to achieve a workable definition of The Regal Pair.

The Disciples Practiced Extreme Righteousness

Teachings on righteousness become mired in ethics, social politics and religious duty. Inculcated in the study of true righteousness are these facets, but they are secondary to God's original meaning. Jesus' teachings and lifestyle encompassed what the Word relegated to this subject. By reviewing Jesus' encounters with those practicing religious righteousness, one sees an image arising from their midst that looks like the pagan god Dagon or an anti-Christ figure. (Anti-Christ images are found in Acts and Peter's writings, as well as John's.)

Gospel writers included the battle between extreme righteousness taught by Jesus and the opposing form taught by religious leaders. Inclusion of these confrontations is not coincidental. Matthew began the display of the battle, while Mark, Luke and John followed. They repeatedly included these confrontations in order to capture, for the believer, the importance of practicing true righteousness—not a false, hollow construct.(Drawing out these passages will reveal the sheer volume they occupy in the total teachings of our Lord, YET, it is frightening while doing so to observe how little time is taken with modern disciples on the subject. Reiteration of the subject matter is scattered throughout the New Testament.)

Paul took up the mantle, and to use modern terminology,

"expunged his relationship to the Pharisees from his resumé!" Disassociation was necessary for him in order to no longer be tainted by their teaching. (It would do well for true believers today to follow suit.)

Extreme Righteousness: The God Kind

Extreme righteousness is the form God practices, and His people should not be associated with less. Bride-ship is determined by this kind of righteousness, "I will betroth you to Me forever; Yes, I will betroth you to Me **In** righteousness ….(Hosea 2:19 NKJV)." Extreme righteousness separates those who really follow Jesus and those who do not!

Only two incidents in the New Testament tell where Pharisees ever stood to assist Jesus. These two incidents represent all such assistance by them during His entire ministry, although they were constantly in His presence. Luke 13:31 tells about a group who warned Jesus of Herod's intent to kill him. The other is the familiar Nicodemus, who inquired of the Lord by night and later stood to reason with his fellow Pharisees about the efficacy of the Son of God.

Relational Vs. Pharisaical

Every other occasion in scripture positions the Scribes and Pharisees on the wrong side of the fence. For all their understanding of scripture, they failed to acknowledge Jesus as the Messiah. Simeon and Anna saw it, why couldn't they? The shepherds and wisemen came to acknowledge Him, but why not the Scribes and Pharisees? They did, however, afford John and Jesus multiple opportunities to teach their disciples and followers true righteousness.

1. Matthew 3:7-13 (NKJV) (John the Baptist is speaking)
    But when he saw many of the Pharisees and Sadducees coming to his baptism, he said to them,

"Brood of vipers! Who warned you to flee from the wrath to come? Therefore bear fruits worthy of repentance, and do not think to say to yourselves, 'We have Abraham as our father.' For I say to you that God is able to raise up children to Abraham from these stones.

2. Matthew 9:11-13 (NKJV)

When the Pharisees saw it, they said to His disciples, 'Why does your Teacher eat with tax collectors and sinners?' When Jesus heard that, He said to them, 'Those who are well have no need of a physician, but those who are sick. But go and learn what this means: I desire mercy and not sacrifice. For I did not come to call the righteous, but sinners, to repentance.'

3. Matthew 15:12-15 (NKJV) (It is interesting to note the Disciples' reaction.)

Do you know that the Pharisees were offended when they heard this saying? But He answered and said, "Every plant which My heavenly Father has not planted will be uprooted. Let them alone. They are blind leaders of the blind. And if the blind leads the blind, both will fall into a ditch."

4. Matthew 16:1-4 (NKJV)

Then the Pharisees and Sadducees came, and testing Him asked that He would show them a sign from heaven. He answered and said to them, When it is evening you say, 'It will be fair weather, for the sky is red'; and in the morning, 'It will be foul weather today, for the sky is red and threatening.' Hypocrites! You know how to discern the face of the sky, but you cannot discern the signs of the times. A wicked and adulterous generation seeks after a sign, and no sign shall be given to it except the sign of the prophet

Jonah. And He left them and departed.

5. Matthew 16:12 (NKJV)

Then they understood that He did not tell them to <u>be-</u><u>ware of the</u> leaven of bread, but of the **doctrine of the Pharisees and Sadducees**.

6. Matthew 21:43-46 (NKJV) (Does this mean the king-dom once was theirs?)

'Therefore I say to you, <u>the **kingdom of God will be taken from you** and given to a nation bearing the fruits of it. And whoever falls on this stone will be broken; but on whomever it falls, it will grind him</u> to powder.' Now when <u>the chief priests and Pharisees heard His parables, they perceived that He was speak-ing of them.</u> But when they sought to lay hands on Him, they feared the multitudes, because they took Him for a prophet.

7. Matt 27:62-64 (NKJV)

On the next day, which followed the Day of Prepara-tion, <u>the chief priests and Pharisees gathered together to Pilate, saying, 'Sir, we remember, while He was still alive, how that deceiver said, 'After three days I will rise.'</u> Therefore command that the tomb be made secure until the third day, lest His disciples come by night and steal Him away, and say to the people, 'He has risen from the dead.'

8. Mark 7:5-9 (NKJV)

Then the **Pharisees and scribes asked Him, 'Why do Your disciples not walk according to the tra-dition of the elders, but eat bread with unwashed hands?' He answered and said to them, 'Well did Isaiah prophesy of you hypocrites, as it is writ-ten: "This people honors Me with their lips, But their heart is far from Me. And in vain they wor-**

**ship Me, Teaching as doctrines the command-
ments of men."**

'For laying aside the commandment of God, you hold
the tradition of men — the washing of pitchers and
cups, and many other such things you do.' And He
said to them, 'All too well you reject the commandment of God, that you may keep your tradition.'

9. Mark 8:15 (NKJV)

'Take heed, beware of the <u>leaven of the Pharisees</u>
and the leaven of Herod.'

10. Luke 5:17-23 (NKJV) (The power of the Lord was
present; they didn't know it)

Now it happened on a certain day, as He was teaching, that there were Pharisees and teachers of the law
sitting by, who had come out of every town of Gali-
lee, Judea, and Jerusalem. And the power of the Lord
was present to heal them.

....the Pharisees began to reason, saying, 'Who is
this who speaks blasphemies? Who can forgive sins
but God alone?' But when Jesus perceived their
thoughts, He answered and said to them, 'Why are
you reasoning in your hearts? Which is easier, to say,
'Your sins are forgiven you,' or to say, 'Rise up and
walk'?"

11. Luke 12:1-3 (NKJV)

In the meantime, when <u>an innumerable multitude</u>
of people had gathered together, so that they trampled
one another, He began to **say to His disciples first of
all, '<u>Beware of the leaven of the Pharisees, which
is hypocrisy.</u> For there is nothing covered that will
not be revealed, nor hidden that will not be known.
Therefore whatever you have spoken in the dark
will be heard in the light, and what you have spo-**

ken in the ear in inner rooms will be proclaimed on the housetops.'

12. John 8:13-20 (NKJV)

The <u>Pharisees therefore said to Him, 'You bear witness of Yourself; Your witness is not true</u>.'

Jesus answered and said to them, 'Even if I bear witness of Myself, My witness is true, for I know where I came from and where I am going; but you do not know where I come from and where I am going. You judge according to the flesh; I judge no one...' Then they said to Him, 'Where is Your Father?' Jesus answered, '**<u>You know neither Me nor My Father</u>. If you had known Me, you would have known My Father also.**' These words Jesus spoke in the treasury, as He taught in the temple; and no one laid hands on Him, for His hour had not yet come.

13. John 8:21-24 (NKJV)

Then Jesus said to them again, '**I am going away, and you will seek Me, and will die in your sin. Where I go you cannot come.**' So the Jews said, 'Will He kill Himself, because He says, "Where I go you cannot come"?' And He said to them, 'You are from beneath; I am from above. You are of this world; I am not of this world. Therefore I said to you that you will die in your sins; for if you do not believe that I am He, you will.'

14. John 18:3 (NKJV)

Then *Judas*, having received a detachment of troops, and officers from **the chief priests and Pharisees**, came there with lanterns, torches, and weapons.

Reactions of Righteousness

Always present, seemingly, always in dispute, always debating, doubting, challenging, forever quoting scripture and citing law, the Pharisees elicited varying responses from Jesus. Once, Jesus called the little children around Him after confronting them (Luke 18:16). Another time, Jesus went away to pray and be alone. Twice, He wept over the condition of Jerusalem and would have called them, "...like a hen doth her brood (Matthew 23:37)." (The whole chapter of Matthew 23 is well worth reading for background on the Pharisees and Jesus' responses.)

Sometimes He did a spectacular healing as the center of His display of extreme righteousness. He did this to show the futility of theological diatribe against the power of action using extreme righteousness.

After one prayer retreat, following battle with them, He gave the sermon on the mount. Luke 6:12 says he left them and went to pray all night (one may conjecture He required being alone with God to be able to continue ministering).

Once He left for Tyre and resorted in a house for a few days, like a spiritual R&R.

If Jesus felt the necessity to confront, rebuke and teach because of encountering huge amounts of error and spiritual depravity, what of true believers today? It is time for spiritual refreshing; it is time for a clear understanding of the truth of God that righteousness and holiness are the most important aspects of the Christian life—radical, extreme righteousness!

CHAPTER FIVE

Kingdom Righteousness

A scepter of righteousness is the scepter of Your Kingdom.
You have loved righteousness and hated lawlessness
Hebrews 1:8-9 (NKJV)

Righteousness and the Kingdom of God are inseparable. When Jesus spoke of righteousness exceeding that of the Pharisees (Matthew 5:20), He forever contrasted Pharisaical type righteousness with Kingdom Righteousness.

The book of Luke (similar to other gospel writers) mentions a cadre of Pharisees in attendance throughout Jesus' parable teaching ministry. It was especially true when He taught on the Kingdom of God. Often they were vehement and angry about what they heard, but Jesus used their presence to add contrast to his teaching.

Kingdom Righteousness has its roots in the King's heart. It is not based on legal standing nor does its justice approximate man's concepts about justice or judgment. Its judgments reach beyond the simple reasoning of courts and legislation, for it is based on emulation of the King: emulation of His inner Being, His ways, His methods, His desire to redeem mankind and grant mercy. This is Kingdom Righteousness, and when it is practiced by His children, it is **not** defined as "filthy rags." It is a rich garment to be worn for His glory.

After several chapters of related Kingdom teaching, Luke brings the reader to the Prodigal Son, where Jesus again characterized Kingdom Righteousness versus man's righteousness. The elder brother epitomized the Pharisees who judged all things according to man's righteousness and had no comprehension of Kingdom principles. The elder brother did all the things required of him. He remained with a respectable earthly task, received his rightful larger portion and stood to profit by outwardly honoring his parent. He did what was expected of him.

> So likewise you, when you have done all those
> things which you are commanded say, 'We are
> unprofitable servants. We have done what was
> our duty to do.'   Luke 17:10 (NKJV)

Kingdom Righteousness is MORE than faithful execution of social order or spiritual tenets, for without entering into the very nature of God, no righteousness exists. In the kingdom, the King rewards those who align with His heart and purpose.

True, in this parable, both were born as earthly sons (but one became a spiritual son when he repented). True, the Prodigal sought to build his own kingdom and failed, but the other did not seek to build anything on a spiritual plain (his anger would not have been directed to the father, otherwise). The older brother, equated with the Pharisees, worked hard at what he considered to be the duties assigned him, yet knew nothing of the heart of the Father. Communication had long since ceased after the father gave away a portion of the money. Had he known the Father's heart, he would have rejoiced at his brother's return. Had he known Kingdom Righteousness, the jealousy he displayed would not have dominated his spirit.

The older brother worked everyday in close proximity to the kingdom but never entered **into** the kingdom of his father (The father's realm had faithful servants, lands, and treasures). The Father conducted himself in line with kingdom principles.

Kingdom Righteousness found expression in the father's words: "It was RIGHT that we should make merry and be glad, for your brother was dead and is alive again, and was lost and is found (Luke 15:32)." The father did what was consistent with his kingdom. The Prodigal hungered and thirsted less from famine than his standing of rightness with his father. This was a spiritual matter. Kingdom Righteousness guarantees one who hungers and thirsts will be filled. The Prodigal came confessing and repenting, asking nothing but a place to serve. Kingdom Righteousness declares those who repent and seek forgiveness of unrighteousness will be forgiven.

The Father placed a ring on his finger and a robe on his back. Kingdom Righteousness restores that which has been lost. The older brother had a portion of wealth and possessed more than enough, but provision without kingdom possession is the plight of the world sans salvation. The older brother stayed OUTSIDE and demanded answers on his terms and on his turf. Unrighteousness always demands legalistic answers. Kingdom Righteousness reached out in love and answered unrighteousness with a higher law and a greater truth.

Power was restored to the son, for his father put a ring on his finger. Restored to his family position, he was clothed with righteousness—for all unrighteousness had been blotted out. He was given a feast of restoration; they killed the "fatted" calf (fat was the part of the peace offering which was given to God as His portion). Kingdom righteousness re-

63

stores its recipients to the family of God! It's a family thing!

Pharisees were listening as they were being described as the older brother. They had given reign to a heart full of jealousy, and their pre-judgment had caused them to be shown as "out of relationship" with the Father.

The Prodigal Son was a parable about Pharisees; the disciples already knew they were family.

> To **you** (the Disciples) it has been given to
> know the mystery of the kingdom of God; but
> to those who are **outside**, all things come in
> parables   Mark 4:11 (NKJV)

Jesus surrounded the Prodigal Son parable with a host of other teachings about Kingdom Righteousness. In Luke 16, the unjust servant was portrayed as receiving a large stewardship (like the older brother) but handling it unfaithfully. The unjust steward's dependence on "unrighteous mammon" revealed a heart not in tune with Kingdom Righteousness. Jesus re-defined for the Pharisees His Fathers concept of unrighteousness. (Today's greatest need is for Divine definition; seekers after God should pray for this!) Unrighteousness was summed as: "What is highly esteemed among men is an abomination in the sight of God (Luke 16:15)."

Should one apply this definition to the modern cadre of believers, here is how it would look: "What the man-controlled church esteems as righteousness is an abomination to God." Worlds of application could be associated with their misanthropy: great buildings, great programs, great evangelistic crusades, great occasions of music and preachment (whatever man determines as "great"), falls under the heading of: "that which is highly esteemed of man." Whatever can be gained through massive offerings and Pharisaical "castings" (as the case with the widow and her mite) is **rarely** viewed by the King as righteous.

Jesus redefined again, by telling the account of the rich man and Lazarus. He applied the gulf that was fixed between them as similar to the spiritual gulf that separated the rich man's unrighteousness from Lazarus' Kingdom Righteousness.

He ended this foray of preaching in parables by summing: "The kingdom of God does not come by observation (it cannot be mimicked); nor will they say, 'See here!' or 'See there!' For indeed, the kingdom of God is within you (Luke 17:20-21)."

For three and one-half chapters before the Prodigal Son parable and an equal number following, Jesus profiled the difference between religious righteousness and Kingdom Righteousness. The difference still stands!

KINGDOM RIGHTEOUSNESS:

> For the kingdom of God is not a matter of eating and drinking, but of **righteousness**, peace and joy in the Holy Spirit.
> Romans 14:17 (NKJV)

Kingdom Righteousness finds definition from the "Branch of Righteousness" (The One so designated to be of the "order of Melchizedek," who is King of Righteousness and Peace). His ministry was (and is) the "ministry of Righteousness."

The following passage speaks of the glory surrounding two kinds of ministry:

> For if the ministry of condemnation had glory, the ministry of righteousness exceeds much more in glory.   2 Corinthians 3:9 (NKJV)

Glory rests upon the Ministry of Righteousness, for out of it flows all ministry. There is no true ministry apart from the ministry of righteousness. The fivefold ministry is a part of it, but the ministry of righteousness is larger than the fivefold ministry. Every action of God issues from it. Every believer has a ministry of righteousness, or he/she is not a believer. Below are some aspects of the ministry of Kingdom Righteousness.

1. Kingdom Righteousness requires that Truth confront falsehood and overcome it. Truth exalted always defines the arena of Righteousness and strikes down all other definitions. The Pharisees represented a "form" of righteousness that did not bear witness to the Kingdom definition; therefore, Jesus attacked it. Speaking in no uncertain terms, He took to task both the error and those who practiced it. Cursory reviews of the gospels reiterate the multiple "affronts" that Jesus made, through His Ministry of Righteousness, to those who taught "another" gospel.

Jesus would not remain silent while unrighteousness was being promoted and practiced. He stood against it. Much of His teachings revolved around defining Righteousness in Kingdom terms, and His definition differed from the constructs of men.

> But seek first the **kingdom of God** and **His righteousness**, and all these things shall be added to you.   Matthew 6:33 (NKJV)

He emphasized the relationship between these two components: the kingdom of God and kingdom righteousness. They are inseparable. No act, regardless of how it is costumed in spiritual garb, will be righteous apart from the kingdom. The Lord, in every case, will be the determinate judge. Thousands of "righteous looking" activities crowd the religious arena, but few bear resemblance to kingdom righteousness.

No work of true righteousness lacks these elements: First, it carries the person of the Father into the task and has His glory in mind. Second, it seeks to establish His truth and kingdom upon the earth. Third, it is always directed to the hearts of mankind in order to restore and build. Fourth, it has no agenda but His. Kingdom Righteousness begins with Him and ends with Him.

Kingdom Righteousness stands to face, endure, and establish the Father's truth, regardless of the suffering, pain, time, cost or self-denial required to accomplish the task. (This is different from man's "works," because no work is righteous that does not first engage His will.)

Kingdom Righteousness allows for no unrighteousness to be excused. It always points to Jesus, who fulfilled and continues to fulfill the righteous requirements of the Law. Kingdom Righteousness pours out of the inner man when linked to the heart of God. (Born in prayer, bathed in His Word, emerging from His will, instructed and concertized by His Spirit.)

Righteousness is a living "organism" in the being of the redeemed! Kingdom Righteousness energized the first Disciples and is alive today in their extended ministry. (Yes, all true ministry is an extension of their initial work.) They sought His righteous judgments and laid bare every design and work which did not seek His goal. To be associated with their ministry is to have the inner-righteousness they possessed in modern vessels. There is no ministry apart from theirs. The current ministry of manipulation does not find its roots in them. But there is more!

2. Kingdom Righteousness expresses itself in Truth being spoken _into_ the world in order for justice and judgment to have clear avenues of execution. Jesus took the Scepter of Righteousness and spoke the Father's Truth into the earth, whether or not that truth encountered favor or adversity. Some things must be spoken into the earth as a witness to the current generation and those to follow. Once spoken, it forever stands as testimony of the light that was available and accountability then will flow from it.

Paralleling Psalms 45 (NKJV), the author of Hebrews in chapter 1, verse 8, says of Jesus:

> 'Your throne, O God is forever and ever; A Scepter of Righteousness is the scepter of Your Kingdom, You have loved righteousness and hated lawlessness; Therefore God, Your God, has anointed You with the oil of gladness more than your companions....

Earlier in this chapter, reference was made to the prophets, for they understood the power of proclaiming truth into the earth. Sometimes they addressed nothing but forest and mountain, but they spoke to them with the authority of heaven. Their Divine Word was needed upon the earth in order to achieve Divine judgment.

When Righteousness rules in one's heart, then the "scepter of righteousness" affords the power to accomplish His works. Without the reign of righteousness, there is no scepter—consequently, the works of religion and man have become expressions of sin and lawlessness. With the Scepter, one rules, both in his personal life and upon the earth.

It is the Scepter of Righteousness that gives credence to "whatsoever you bind on earth shall be bound in heaven." Prosperity and every covenant blessing comes through Righteousness. Psalms 112 declares those who fear the Lord are known and blessed by their Righteousness. Promises such as one's descendants being mighty on earth, wealth and riches being in the house, never being shaken by circumstances in life, never being afraid of evil tiding, having a heart steadfast in the Lord, having one's desires over his enemies, lifting his head in honor, and never being forgotten are all pronounced with this truth: "His righteousness endures forever!"

Weakened by the "infidels of the gospel," who service

multitudes with platefuls of spiritual "husks which the swine eat," congregations have become spiritually emaciated. Christendom longs to be embraced with the love of the Father who invests robes of righteousness and rings of authority upon prodigals in repentance. Christendom repeatedly hears the story and continually misses the point. The Prodigal was forever adherent to the rule of the father from the moment of acceptance forward. What his father willed, he willed. What the father favored, he favored. His authority was always to establish the word of his Father.

Believers must take the "scepter of righteousness" and begin pronouncing the Father's will upon the earth, declaring with Prodigal fervor that things have changed because their heart has changed! Righteousness Rules!

> Behold a King will reign in righteousness and
> princes will rule with justice.
> > Isaiah 32:1(NKJV)

When righteousness occupies its place in the heart of the believer, it is not an option whether he or she will rule and reign. Righteousness reigns! Inherent in righteousness is the power to reign. His people demonstrate this power and resource in Righteousness, for it is their "effectual, fervent prayer" that avails MUCH.

3. Kingdom Righteousness presupposes Divine Appointment. Upon the earth, as people of God conduct their lives in righteousness, it gives opportunity for the Lord to bring others into their lives. Righteousness draws righteousness to itself. There is no basis for fellowship apart from that formed around people of righteousness. Churches lie in the wreckage of their community, built on flesh rather than righteousness. Ecclesiastical circles may use networking, pyramids of advancement, "forums of the likeminded (conventions, special feature speakers and alumnus)," but God uses

69

the magnetism of Righteousness to draw together those who are His. Enclaves of Righteousness are being formed upon the earth in preparation for the soon coming King. These fellowships are based on a mutual hungering and thirsting for more righteousness and holiness.

The only corporate worship or fellowship available to end-time believers is that which is based on this premise: Fellowship arises among hearts made comrade in righteousness. Churches and fellowships have totally disregarded this premise; therefore, they seek to be a universal house, not an upper room! Upper room fellowship was the path to inclusion for the early church; upper room fellowship was based on Kingdom righteousness. Strange events surrounded their unity; when unrighteousness raised it head, unrighteousness was carried out in coffins! Righteousness has a negative and a positive bent.

Righteousness draws mankind to the Kingdom. Jesus, "The Branch of Righteousness," and One created after the "order of Melchizedek (the King of Righteousness)" said, " If I be lifted up, I WILL draw all men unto me (John 12:32, NKJV)." Righteousness is characterized by its magnetic drawing of those who should be saved. (When Jesus resides in the human heart, the magnetism of His presence belongs to the believer.) The Disciples were prime examples of this principle.

It was not the charisma of Peter that drew five thousand converts; it was righteousness which did the drawing. It was not the persuasiveness of Philip that won a Eunuch. It was not the cleverness of Paul that gave a world-presence to the Kingdom; it was righteousness drawing. There is no drawing power of lasting dimension aside from kingdom righteousness. It was not Moravian zeal that caused them to move across continents and enslave themselves in order to win slaves; it was righteousness drawing.

Personality, charm, charisma, promotion, media swill or clever marketing will never have the eternal results found within the drawing of righteousness. Holy men and women, moved by God, are drawn into relationships and opportunities that cannot be afforded the most intense networker!

Alas, the church has suffered the same lot as ancient Jerusalem in Isaiah's time.

> How the faithful city has become a harlot!
> It WAS full of justice (the realm of righteousness) **Righteousness** lodged in it, But now murderers...
> Your silver has become dross (tarnished, not bright) Your wine mixed with water (watered down mixture) Your princes are rebellious (leadership) And companion of thieves (fellowship with unrighteousness) everyone loves bribes (large offerings and favors) and follows after rewards (ministerial perks)...

(The Lord speaks in verse 25)

> I will thoroughly purge away your dross, and take away your alloy. I will restore your judges (God chose judges, man chose kings) as at the first and your counselors as at the beginning (of whom Jesus is the Mightiest) AFTERWARD you shall be called the **city of RIGHTEOUSNESS**, the Faithful city Zion shall be redeemed with justice, AND HER PENITENTS WITH **RIGHTEOUSNESS**
> Isaiah 1:21-27 (NKJV)

At this very hour, the Lord is drawing together His people to be a city of righteousness and its citizens possessors of kingdom righteousness. A corporate blessing is only available at the place of righteousness. No religious group need seek the blessing of God without the rule of kingdom righteousness.

4. Kingdom Righteousness only comes through the Holy Spirit.

Just as Jesus is the mediator between earth and heaven, the Spirit is His mediator from heaven to earth. The passage below is situated at the end of a long treatise by Jesus to His disciples concerning matters of the kingdom. He addressed what they would encounter in the future and how they were to react. Near the end, He taught:

> 'And when He (the Spirit) comes, He will con-
> vict the world of sin, and of <u>righteousness</u>, and
> of judgment: of sin, because they do not be-
> lieve in Me, of <u>righteousness</u> because I go to
> My Father and you see Me no more, of judg-
> ment, because the ruler of this world is
> judged...When He, the Spirit of truth, has come
> He will guide you into all truth; for He will
> not speak on His own authority, but whatever
> He hears He will speak; and He will tell you
> things to come. He will glorify Me, for He will
> take of what is mine and declare it to you.'
>
> John 16:8-14.(NKJV)

The range of meaning commentators have designated to this passage is horrendous, but for the purposes of this book, it is necessary to examine the passage as an integral part of a total message delivered to Jesus' disciples. What is basically said is: "the Holy Spirit will come and confront the world about sin, righteousness and judgment." Spoken in modern parlance, one might speak of the Holy Spirit initiating a spiri-tual revolution.

Spiritual Revolution

Framed against a Pharisee-Scribe education, this message was indeed revolutionary. It still is, given the current backdrop of spiritual illiteracy found in most congregations.

The Holy Spirit desired to speak through the Disciples the same kinds of things Jesus had been speaking. Jesus spoke what He heard from the Father; the Disciples must speak what they heard through the Spirit. Sometimes the message from heaven was simply to correct false teaching or confront unrighteousness. Unfortunately, this was not a "one time" correction connection. Sadly, it is a correction which now must be carried both to the world and the church of the world. (Jesus confronted error in the established religion of His day and that confrontation continues.)

Conviction of Sin

Conviction is the work of the Spirit, not the work of the church. Almost all religious bodies have a strong sense of the conviction of sin and the conviction of the judgment of the evil one; they lack knowledge of the Holy Spirit's work in conviction of righteousness.

He alone is the convictor! His work in convicting of sin is to bring the reality of sin to the consciousness of the sinner, to get that reality to the forefront of life until he or she is unable to avoid dealing with it. When the reality of sin is manifested, then repentance toward God can take place. One's personal agreement with the Spirit, about the matter of sin and reproof of those sins, leads to change. The Spirit moves alongside the sinner until there is consensus. He then brings the gift of grace and applies the blood of Jesus. The people of the world have been wrong in their estimation of Jesus and His work of grace. Holy Spirit conviction redefines sin and gives the convictee eyes that see. The initial work of the Spirit brings further conviction.

73

Conviction of Righteousness

Yet, there is more! The world has been wrong about the Spirit's conviction of righteousness as well. The convicting power of the Spirit regarding righteousness is at work. He begins by projecting true kingdom righteousness on the wall of the heart, setting His definition before the believer so he or she must deal with it. Again, He calls for a change! He offers the gift of righteousness, but it is offered in the same manner as salvation. The hearer must repent and receive it. The hearer must become involved by faith and reach for that which is offered. He must make true righteousness part of his inner man; consensus must again be reached with the Spirit. The true believer must embrace Him. Just as emphatically as one says, "I am the redeemed of the Lord," one must now say, " I am the righteousness of Christ."

Conviction of Judgment

Yet there is more! The world's construct of judgment has been in error also. The Holy Spirit has come to convince, reprove, convict and bring about understanding and change again, this time concerning judgment. As this relates to the believer, he is now able to declare, "Greater is He that is within Me, than he that is in the world (I John 4:4)." The believer now knows the evil one is judged and cannot exercise power in his life unless he allows it.

Jesus declared spiritual war on three fronts. He spoke to sin, righteousness and judgment, categories by which His messages can be catalogued. The Holy Spirit will take these areas to any person who will open himself or herself.

Sadly, most believers deny the Holy Spirit access to His office. Just as He brought forgiveness and cleansing to the believer's inward parts by salvation, He wishes to establish Holiness and Righteousness as the inner fabric of the believer. Multitudes have not allowed His work! Theology has sought to rob the Spirit of His office. Debating endlessly and writing continuously about the qualitative aspects of righteousness (breaking righteousness down to theological terms such as "retributive" versus "restorative righteousness" etc.), they render chilling fingers to what should be a glowing flame.

Declaring an automatic imputation of righteousness in man at the moment of salvation, the church and theology have sought to close the dialogue between man and the Spirit.

The Spirit keeps re-opening that dialogue in these last days, and holiness and righteousness will be the next great revival to sweep Kingdom saints. The Holy Spirit is bringing conviction of righteousness to the forefront of the true church. Holiness and Righteousness **will** bring to Christ, a spotless Bride! The last voice of History will be the combined voice of the Spirit and the Bride, "and the Spirit and the Bride say come (Revelation 22:17)."

Nothing of lasting value on earth can be accomplished without the Spirit. The worldly church, however, continues to think it can operate successfully without Him. Evangelical churches have emphasized "their rights and privileges as believers," but none dare talk of the "rights and privileges" of the Spirit. Such sovereignty is too great for those who plan and execute their plans according to men!

Righteousness Restores

Righteousness in the believer is not to be a theological term applied to "a position" in Christ; it is to be the connecting link to the Righteousness found in the Father and the Son. Adam knew the God of holiness and righteousness as a person. The Holy Spirit seeks to restore every believer to this knowledge. Adam needed no other credential than the inner witness of The Regal Pair. When Adam sinned, the built in plumb line of the Pair (righteousness and holiness) was removed from him, and he was LOST without it. No man may

75

approach God without the Regal Pair.

Adam was born into a family relationship. (An understanding of Adam's original state is important in order to determine personal restoration.) Centuries ago, preachers understood and preached from such a position.

Here is Mitchell's synopsis of a preacher of renown, an early American pastor and evangelist, Jonathan Edwards, an integral part of the Great Awakening.

Jonathan Edwards believed pre-sin Adam possessed righteousness:

> Adam, however, differed from most men in one important way: he possessed a unique will that was <u>inclined toward </u>righteousness. Edwards was convinced that two types of principles were instilled in Adam's will. The first were natural, or inferior, ones. These are seen in self-love, and other such desires and inclinations as belong to the nature of man—the Bible often refers to these as the Flesh. The second, superior principles were spiritual ones. Chief among these are divine love, <u>man's righteousness, and true holiness</u>. Since they are supernatural principles, 'These immediately depend on man's union and communion with God, or divine communications and influences of God's Spirit.'
> Living in the garden of Eden, Adam enjoyed the privileges of the spiritual principles, which, 'were given to possess the throne, and maintain an absolute dominion in the heart....' [1]

In order for the redeemed to be restored completely, conviction of sin must be followed by conviction **to** righteousness. Sin robbed man of his righteousness. God will restore to the believer all that was taken from Adam. This is more than a personality adjustment. Righteousness is not just a moral-ethical aspect restored in a believer; it is more than positional "rightness" toward God and Man; it is the foundation of harmony found in open communication with the throne of God. (Restored Righteousness takes dominion in the heart. Edwards knew and preached this. The community of believers in the Twenty-first Century cannot afford to believe less than those of the 1700's.)

Two steps past the fiery guard at the garden's gate, if a newsman could have questioned Adam asking, "What in the garden do you miss the most?" his answer would have been, "Fellowship with God." His greatest loss through sinning was his break in fellowship with His Father. Unrighteousness breaks fellowship; righteousness perpetuates fellowship. This is a family of God matter!

Kingdom Righteousness is a family thing. Just as Christian families discuss what behavior is acceptable to them and what the family stands for in the larger social arena, the family of God has its familial expectations. Righteousness, then, is not so much the absence of certain behaviors or the meeting of some standard of propriety, it is the living out of one's life in fellowship within the family of God. It is understanding Kingdom Righteousness.

> You were taught, with regard to your former way of life, to put off your old self, which is being corrupted by its deceitful desires; to be made new in the attitude of your minds; and to put on the new self, <u>created to be **like God** in true righteousness and holiness</u>.
>
> Ephesians 4:22-24 (NIV)

Righteousness on earth is family preparation for the lifestyle of heaven!

> But in keeping with his promise we are look-
> ing forward to a new heaven and a new earth,
> the home of righteousness.
>
> 2 Peter 3:13 (NIV)

Righteousness is still a family matter. When one sees himself or herself as the bride of Christ, then Hosea's prophecy begins to form a beautiful promise.

> 'In that day,' declares the LORD,
> 'you will call me "my husband;"
> You will no longer call me "my master".'
>
> Hosea 2:16 (NIV)

> 'I will betroth you to me forever; I will be-
> troth you in righteousness and justice, in love
> and compassion. I will betroth you in faithful-
> ness, and you will acknowledge the LORD.'
>
> Hosea 2:19-20 (NIV)

Righteousness is at the inner core of membership in the family of God! It is what the family of God is built upon. It is an inseparable companion to holiness, and in order to function within the family unit, this gift of righteousness must take a higher position than it has been afforded in pulpit and pew! Organized religion, by seeking to confine the work of the Spirit to the affirmation of their works, has failed to allow the Spirit His convicting power in righteousness.

Watchman Nee, the great Chinese pastor and prophet, addressed the issue:

> Our righteousness before God is not depen-
> dant on our conduct, but on Christ Himself...
> Righteousness is a person; It is not a thing...it
> is not some dead object.[2]

Righteous Judgment

Judgment now lies at the door! The Spirit has been sent

to convict the world of judgment. They who have been wrong about sin and righteousness also have been wrong about judgment. Judgment is the reward of righteousness. It's a family matter!

> We are bound to thank God always for you, brethren, as it is fitting, because your faith grows exceedingly, and the love of every one of you all abounds toward each other, so that we ourselves boast of you among the churches of God for your patience and faith in all your persecutions and tribulations that you endure, which is manifest evidence of the **righteous judgment** of God, that you may be counted worthy of the **kingdom of God**, for which you also suffer; since it is **a righteous thing** with God <u>to repay with tribulation those who trouble you</u>, and to give you who are troubled rest with us when the Lord Jesus is revealed from heaven with His mighty angels, in flaming fire taking vengeance on those who do not know God, and on those who do not obey the gospel of our Lord Jesus Christ.
>
> 2 Thessalonians 1:3-8 (NKJV)

It is righteous judgment that Jesus will exact on satan's worldly kingdom in the last days. His judgment is on behalf of His righteous people. Because righteousness has been loosed upon the earth by these Righteous people, the unrighteous live without excuse. Salt savors still, lights shine still, living water flows from bellies still, anointing breaks the yoke still, miracles continue still and the voice of martyrs cry still— for righteous judgment. Righteous judgment is the nature of righteousness. It is this "righteous kingdom judgment" of which the Spirit convicts the world. Revelation will be proven correct when the final days appear, for the Unrighteous will curse God for their tribulation but still refuse to repent. They will blame God for acts of the devil and allow twisted theology to penetrate their mind set, but they will refuse to be convicted by the Spirit.

Because the "righteousness ones" are Spirit-determined, their lives have already judged every sin, weakness, fault, error, misdirection, carnality, trespass and misappropriation. They are accustomed to judgment, for they began it in their own life. By putting themselves under the cleansing blood, their remaining judgment is a reward judgment. These who have judged every aspect of the world around them righteously and chosen a path that often caused them pain, suffering, persecution, indignity, sorrow, death, poverty and misunderstanding—will rise to Judge others at the end time.

Righteous people know what the Spirit has warned, convicted and sought for the hearts of a world without God. They have been present when the world rejected that conviction. Their judgeship will be a kingdom judgeship. This is a kingdom matter, and what counts is every soul who has not been judged by the Spirit will be judged by those of the Spirit!

Work for the Righteous

It is time for the Holy Ones to search out passages about end-time judgment and begin to pray those things into being. These catastrophic events are not options which can be changed at whim; they are credible events which must take place before the Lord Jesus can come back to earth. As difficult as this word may seem, let it be remembered that all the matters of judgment spoken in the Word are matters for the righteous. In order for Righteousness to be fulfilled, these events must come to pass. Every end-time event recorded in the word of God should be a matter of prayer. It is the Righteous prayer that avails much.

Heaven already has witnessed the painful judgment of unrighteous angels (Rev. 12). One third of the angel population was cast out of the kingdom at one time.

Today, greater numbers than the angels shall suffer as kingdom righteousness is fulfilled. Intercession should start in order for these judgments to begin. Saints upon the earth must join voice with those under the altar and cry for Him to begin the promised transaction! A world of rival religions lays coiled to bring war against the Righteous. The Righteous stand in battle array, armed with helmets of salvation, swords of the Spirit, breastplates of righteousness, girded with truth and shod with the plan of the gospel. Judgment is about to be wrought by the spiritually armed Righteous.

Such judgments, however, are an impetus for winning those who must face them. Knowing that certain judgment lies ahead for friends, relatives, neighbors and acquaintances is a propelling force to seek the lost both at home and abroad.

End-times are exciting times for the Righteous. Knowing that satan has been judged and his followers are facing similar judgment is a powerful rock to be used by the redeemed against the Goliaths of death, hell and the judgment. The Righteous Ones hold no fear or trepidation, for they are MORE than conquerors through Him who loves them. He who has been judged by God's Righteous One knows it is now time for those who have not—to be judged.

Short time remains for the Unrighteous to deal with the convicting presence of the Spirit. Putting before their consciences the certain matter of impending judgment should once again be the topic of the fivefold ministry. Intercession should begin by calling for these convicting arenas to increase in number, intensity and speed. The true church must cry out, "O God, turn up the volume, increase the intensity, step up the pressure, cause conviction of sin, righteousness and judgment to take place worldwide. Do it NOW!" Let this message be heard from every corner and seep through every crevice:

> But in accordance with your hardness and your impenitent heart you are treasuring up for yourself wrath in the day of wrath and <u>revelation of the righteous judgment</u> of God, who will render to each one according to his deeds: eternal life to those who by patient continuance in doing good seek for glory, honor, and immortality; but to those who are self-seeking and do not obey the truth, <u>but obey unrighteousness</u> — indignation and wrath.
>
> Romans 2:5-8 (NKJV)

All judgment is kingdom based. Two kinds of people roam the earth: Those in the kingdom and those outside it. Those inside the kingdom, through the Spirit, seek the will and work of the Father, and those outside do not. Regardless of the assurances of well meaning clergy and vast numbers of their misled followers, the test in the kingdom is righteousness. Pharisees may still exist, but kingdom righteousness still exceeds their kind and progressively moves toward the throne of reward. Awareness of this dichotomy must be intensified in the last days. Parlaying with interfaith movements, which seek to justify adherence to all faiths equally, is the game of imposters, not the people of righteousness! Lines have been drawn in heaven and in earth. Regardless of the cost, righteousness will pay it. Regardless of the roadblocks satan seeks to raise, the righteous will overcome them. Righteous Ones are rising up and will again be heard, for these are their days— the judgment of the nations belongs to them!

5. Finally, kingdom righteousness has to do with glory. Paul teaches that kingdom righteousness gives God glory.

But God has chosen the foolish things of the world to put to shame the wise, and God has chosen the weak things of the world to put to shame the things which are mighty; and the base things of the world and the things which are despised God has chosen, and the things which are not, to bring to nothing the things that are, that no flesh should glory in His presence. But of Him you are in Christ Jesus, who became for us wisdom from God—and righteousness and sanctification and redemption—that, as it is written, "He who glories, let him glory in the LORD.

1 Corinthians 1:27-31 (NKJV)

Paul also taught that the Ministry of Righteousness also has glory.

For if the ministry of condemnation had glory, the ministry of righteousness exceeds much more in **glory**. For even what was made glorious had no glory in this respect, because of the glory that excels. For if what is passing away was glorious, what remains is much more glorious.   2 Corinthians 3:9-11 (NKJV)

Kingdom Righteousness has a glory factor. Paul taught, in the first passage, that all righteousness is based in Christ, and He alone gets the glory. The same is true in the second passage, for adherents to kingdom righteousness find that Righteousness has a built in glory.

Those who are wise shall shine
Like the brightness of the firmament,
And those who turn many to righteousness
Like the stars forever and ever.

Daniel 12:3 (NKJV)

83

God's glory will only rest on those who are Holiness and Righteousness Beings, just as He is. Their inner core identifies with His, and His glory is upon them. Many people, good people, who manifest nothing of the righteousness of God in their lives have been promised a glory-filled eternity; when, in fact, it is an impossible promise. Just like sin has built-in judgment, righteousness has built-in glory.

Recently, a Bible teacher, standing before a relatively large mid-week crowd, declared, "You are the ones who bring the glory into the house of God," pointing her finger here and there toward various non-descript persons in the audience. Her point of emphasis was clear: If there was to be glory in the house, they would have to bring it. Her preachments were only partially true. Her pronouncement was directed to a general church audience and bore no qualification of righteousness. When preachments like this are heard, there rises up in the righteous hearer a desire to call out, "No, No, No, for without righteousness in their life, it will be a false glory which will be brought in." Unfortunately for many organizations, the false glory is all they have beheld. Believers do not have to "bring" glory; when the Righteous assemble, the glory comes! It's a family matter!

CHAPTER SIX

Enclaves of Righteousness

But what does the divine response say to him?
"I have reserved for Myself seven thousand men
who have not bowed the knee to Baal."
Romans 11:4 (NKJV)

At this very hour, there are enclaves of just men and women who have not bowed their knee to Religious Baal. Often referred to as the "remnant," their place in history has been fixed. "Remnant" they are indeed, for they have been torn from society, ripped from the pursuits of the flesh, cut from the failing throws of religion, severed from the mediocrity of what is called "Christian." They have been scorned by those searching for success (like some piece of cloth left on a bolt— considered as "of little use" by those who make judgments according to their plans and being considered "odd," by those measuring by their own standards), cast aside, like some "off-scouring." Solitary after the "choice ones" have been lifted to "favor," these "remnants" pray, seek God in the secret place. They watch spiritually, intercede, determine by Divine Judgment where they are to reside and what will be priority for their lives. Pockets of spiritual power, they are hidden to the world and strategically scattered about the globe. They are enclaves seeking only the Father's will. The Father knows everyone of them well.

Enclaves may range in size from one individual on a Patmos-like Island, to many who have chosen to group together. They are known by the Spirit, even though they may be unknown to men.

Elijah, who felt he was the last man standing for God (the only one who cared about the things of God), experienced the truth concerning enclaves while pleading against Israel. God revealed He had special cadres of souls, who lived holy and righteous lives, and He knew the address of each of them. They numbered in the thousands. Known as the "holy ones," their righteousness qualified them to be called, "the reserves."

Enclaves Visited

Individuals or groups dwelling apart from their secular fellows, bent upon serving only God and dedicated to being used exclusively by the Lord, become islands of holiness and righteousness in a sea of compromise. Yet, God's seven thousand formed a corporate body, an army of battlers, a Congregation of Light and a reservoir of spiritual understanding in a world of darkness and ignorance. They are repositories of power in an exhausted generation.

Enclaves may be constituted by any number, from one to groups of two or three to larger communities. The numbers do not matter, what matters is that they are the "separated ones." Their lives are the equivalent of Noah and Lot in Peter's writings. They are the ones who are the **owners** of holiness and righteousness amid a world having lost all sense of those qualities. (2 Peter 2:5-9 see below)

Noah and Lot, the Righteous Twins

Noah and Lot—who would have imagined their linkage, but Simon (under the guidance of the Spirit) placed them together as examples of enclaves of righteousness dwelling in worlds gone mad. Their presence in their several societies made them appear to be "out of step;" but alas, they were the only ones "in step" with God. Each were dubbed "righteous," though living in places sold out to unrighteousness. The issue is not, "Why did God call them righteous?" so much as, "What did they possess that made them enclaves of righteousness?"

Righteous Noah

Hebrews discussed some of the aspects a reader needs to know.

> But without faith it is impossible to please Him, for he who comes to God must believe that He is, and that He is a rewarder of those who diligently seek Him. By faith Noah, being divinely warned of things not yet seen, moved with godly fear, prepared an ark for the saving of his household, by *which he condemned the world* and became heir of the righteousness which is according to faith.
>
> Hebrews 11:6-7 (NKJV)

Simon Peter added to the bank of knowledge these words:

> For Christ also suffered once for sins, the just for the unjust, that He might bring us to God, being put to death in the flesh but made alive by the Spirit, by whom also He went and preached to the spirits in prison, who formerly were disobedient, when once the Divine longsuffering waited in the days of Noah, while

87

the ark was being prepared, in which a few, that is, eight souls, were saved through water. There is also an antitype which now saves us— baptism (not the removal of the filth of the flesh, but the answer of a good conscience toward God), through the resurrection of Jesus Christ, who has gone into heaven and is at the right hand of God, angels and authorities and powers having been made subject to Him.

1 Peter 3:18-22 (NKJV)

Simon joined together two people who faced similar circumstances, Noah and Lot:

For if God did not spare the angels who sinned, but cast them down to hell and delivered them into chains of darkness, to be reserved for judgment; and did not spare the ancient world, but saved Noah one of eight people, **a preacher of righteousness**, bringing in the flood on the world of the ungodly; and turning the cities of Sodom and Gomorrah into ashes, condemned them to destruction, making them an example to those who afterward would live ungodly; and delivered **righteous** Lot, who was oppressed by the filthy conduct of the wicked (**for that righteous man**, dwelling among them, tormented his **righteous** soul from day to day by seeing and hearing their lawless deeds) — then the Lord knows how to deliver the godly out of temptations and to reserve the unjust under punishment for the day of judgment, and especially those who walk according to the flesh in the lust of uncleanness and despise authority. They are presumptuous, self-willed. They are not afraid to speak evil of dignitaries, whereas angels, who are greater in power and might, do not bring a reviling accusation against them before the Lord. But these, like natural brute beasts made to be caught and destroyed, speak evil of the things they do not understand, and will utterly perish in their own corruption, and will receive the wages of unrighteousness

2 Peter 2: 4-13 (NKJV)

Self-evident in these passages are two major premises: First, the Lord ALWAYS has an enclave of righteousness available to the world, furnishing an example of how things should be in the life of the Kingdom; secondly, they act as the basis for judgment to those who refuse to emulate their example. Two kinds of people are in the earth, those who follow the example of righteousness and those who refuse. Righteousness is still the plumb-line!

Within the aforementioned scriptures are several underlined or italicized passages which are places of special emphasis for this study. The initial passage shows by Noah's example, two aspects to be observed: First, he chose to hear and believe God in a world that neither heard nor regarded Him, thereby becoming the agent of "righteous" condemnation. Yes, there is a righteous (demanded, deserved) judgment for those who refuse the example. They earn the "wages of unrighteousness." Sin has built-in judgment. Righteousness has built-in justice. Second, Noah became, by his own faith, an "heir of righteousness." The building of the ark did not make him an heir. Nothing Noah could have done apart from faith would have made him "heir." He was a part of the "Family of Righteousness." The same is true with one who is righteous today. It is a family affair.

Since Noah lived many years before Jesus, his inheritance was preserved for him. He also became a significant source of judgment to be used by Jesus in His ministry. Without Noah and his family acting as an enclave of righteousness, those who perished would not have seen the crucified Lord of Glory when he triumphed over death. Those condemned ones SAW the "righteousness of God," in person. Noah stood as an anti-type of redemption. How? He was the righteous reason for judgment; Jesus was the righteous reason for salvation!

Righteous Lot

Noah is joined to Lot creating the righteous duo. These two men merge in Scripture. It is always interesting in the Bible to observe the people God joins together for exemplary reference (Job and Daniel are good examples.). Both these men saved their families and themselves from destruction. (It is to be noted that Lot's wife was not delivered because her heart was not focused on the journey. She did not obey the Lord with exactness, which is important to note. Whether her looking back enabled her to see the judgment fall, to see the extent of the judgment or because she longed not to leave, one is not told. The result of disobedience carried a terrific price. It will be the same in the Twenty-first Century.)

Noah is an easier example than Lot for some people, but it doesn't matter about man's preferences. God deemed them both "righteous" and perhaps for different reasons. Noah believed God and PREACHED righteousness. He preached, not just righteous acts, but inner-core-repentance and faith toward God, on every occasion he had. There are few preachers of righteousness even today! Inner-core-righteousness was not received by Noah's audience because he had no converts from his messages—the last days shall be as the days of Noah!

> This is the genealogy of Noah. Noah was a just (righteous) man, perfect in his generations. Noah walked with God. And Noah begot three sons: Shem, Ham, and Japheth. The earth also was corrupt before God, and the earth was filled with violence. So God looked upon the earth, and indeed it was corrupt; for all flesh had corrupted their way on the earth. And God said to Noah, 'The end of all flesh has come before Me, for the earth is filled with violence through them; and behold, I will destroy them with the earth.'   Genesis 6:9-13 (NKJV)

The Lord supplied, in advance, evidence of his intentions—to destroy the earth and its populations. Preparation for this occasion took several years, a point of difference with Lot.

> And as it was in the days of Noah, so it will be also in the days of the Son of Man: They ate, they drank, they married wives, they were given in marriage, until the day that Noah entered the ark, and the flood came and destroyed them all. Likewise as it was also in the days of Lot: They ate, they drank, they bought, they sold, they planted, they built; but on the day that Lot went out of Sodom it rained fire and brimstone from heaven and destroyed them all. Even so will it be in the day when the Son of Man is revealed.   Luke 17:26-31 (NKJV)

Lot was not distinguished as a preacher of righteousness. Lot was more passive, even though his soul was vexed by what he saw and what he heard. Nevertheless, an outcry against the city came before God. Perhaps some enclave of the righteous, somewhere, observed the "goings on" of Sodom and cried against it. Abraham, upon learning of its fate, interceded for the home of Lot and hence the famous bargaining. Righteous men and women were the bargaining tools. Alas, not fifty, not forty-five, not even ten could be found in Sodom's gates. The hunt for men of righteousness may not yield better numbers today! The difference between salvation and decimation always turns on the presence or absence of righteousness!

Peter's Sovereign Truths

Evidence in Peter's verses indicate three sovereign truths: First, righteous men take their surrounding seriously and are often vexed by the "goings on" around them. Let the reader imagine the circumstances Lot found himself in while enduring a homosexual/ bisexual city, where elicit sex was the characterizing descriptor for the community, such could have been featured on the chamber of commerce brochure. Further, imagine trying to raise children in such an environ with limited agreement from one's spouse. Understand the Lot family dilemma as their children began marrying local men. Second, Lot's righteousness extended to his sons-in-law, but in the end, their own will prevailed leaving him with his two daughters. Third, God can and will deliver an enclave of the righteous ahead of judgment. He did it then, and He will do so now.

It is to be noted that both Noah and Lot played a key part in their own deliverance and in standing as righteous examples. By so doing, God was justified in His drastic actions. Faith-Righteousness always has a deliverer!

Ancient and Modern Enclaves

"Will He find faith on the earth?" was a valid question then, just as it is now in the last days. There are enclaves today of individuals, families and groups, who are similar to

Noah and Lot. They are scattered globally. God knows them and knows the righteousness in their inner core. They may not be present at the formal prayer service, the evangelistic outreach, or be "involved" like others in standard church fare, BUT they are "alive and well." They stand as living witnesses to the populace facing the soon coming righteous judgment of the world.

Seven thousand souls were unknown to Elijah because they were not in the "usual" spiritual places. (Seven thousand is the perfect number multiplied a thousand fold.) Seven thousand souls who were strong in the Lord, who had not reached out for iniquity were alive and well. Seven thousand saints, who were not under the scepter of unrighteousness for they determined within their hearts, that no matter how much pressure was exerted upon them, they would not bow to Baal or kiss his image. They were strong souls who knew what it was to hear God's voice. They bathed their actions in prayer and sought His sovereignty even when to do so was upon pain of death. Romans eleven says they were reserved by God for Himself, meaning they were His special possession. Are there seven thousand today who have not made man's created religion their husband or possessor?

Elijah's Three

When Elijah received this revelation from God, several things were at play in his life. First, he declared to God that his zeal for God had gotten him to a miserable state.

> 'I have been very zealous for the LORD God of hosts; because the children of Israel have forsaken Your covenant, torn down Your altars, and killed Your prophets with the sword. I alone am left; and they seek to take my life.'
>
> 1 Kings 19:14 (NKJV)

Something should be noted here, any of the seven thousand could have said, "I alone am left; and they seek to take my life." Scripture does not reveal that any of them knew the other. Elijah was a human experiencing the agony of being a "wanted" man for doing "the will of God." Many today, have similar feelings. Second, Elijah was replaced as the chief prophet after this experience. He had fled to the Mountain of God and was required by God to return home the same way he came. The Lord arranged some Divine encounters for him along the way. One of those encounters was with Elisha. Scripture does not tell whether Elijah knew Elisha existed before this time. Elisha developed his stature with God apart from Elijah's assistance and became a man who, in all his ministry, did awesome deeds of righteousness. Third, Elijah was in a spiritual war with his inward man. God was not just comforting Elijah with the knowledge that there were seven thousand who stood in reserve; He was chiding Elijah for thinking that the whole of the Kingdom depended upon him. God had seven thousand who were zealous for Him, one of whom was named Elisha. The Lord showed Elijah just a few of the seven thousand, but any of them could have been like Elisha, for all of them were God's private possession.

> Blessed are those you choose and bring near
> to live in your courts! We are filled with the
> good things of your house of your holy temple.
> You answer us with <u>awesome deeds of righteousness</u>...   Psalms 65:4-5 (NIV)

Enclaves are like that—they operate under a Divine Order unlike religious institutions. God is limitless, so the scope of their spiritual universe is as large as His. In seeking His face and being willing to draw closer to His presence, they fulfill the scripture, "*I will* show you great and mighty things which you do not know (Jeremiah 33:3)." Just as the Lord

94

answers by "awesome deeds of righteousness," their response to the world is to be like Him. They seek to bring such deeds upon the earth. Unlike "righteous acts," these deeds are drawn from the righteous heart of God through the righteous heart of man directed to bless or curse the earth. These "directed acts of God's Righteousness" find entrance through the co-operative righteousness of the "holy ones."

Many of those who are among the "reserves" know that the Lord is drawing them into a greater dimension of His presence, a place where the possibility of their being "drawn back into the earth world" is diminished or eliminated. In this royal room, they are able to intercede and call things upon the earth with deft wisdom. Open to them are realms of glory and spiritual scope not available to the "passing prayer."

Elisha's acts superceded those of Elijah as a double portion supercedes a single one. God is able to go beyond double for the heart willing to receive it. These Last Days will see persons (individuals) like Elisha, and corporately like many of the seven thousand, reach into realms of the Spirit unknown to former days. "Awesome Deed of Righteousness," (which is a noun form) will bring about a spiritual day that will eclipse that of the Disciples.

These, who are willing to "lay down their lives," say like Paul:

> We put no stumbling block in anyone's path, so that our ministry will not be discredited. Rather, as **servants of God** we commend ourselves in every way: in great endurance; in troubles, hardships and distresses; in beatings, imprisonments and riots; in hard work, sleepless nights and hunger; in purity, understanding, patience and kindness; in the Holy Spirit and in sincere love; in truthful speech and in

the power of God; with **weapons of righteous-ness** <u>in the right hand and in the left</u>; through glory and dishonor, bad report and good report; genuine, yet regarded as impostors; known, yet regarded as unknown; dying, and yet we live on; beaten, and yet not killed; sorrowful, yet always rejoicing; poor, yet making many rich; having nothing, and yet possessing everything.

2 Corinthians 6:3-10 (NIV)

In these last days, there are enclaves of the Lord being assembled unto Him. In Northwest Arkansas, several families occupy land to which the Spirit led them after many years of intensive prayer. For twelve years they have prayed, worked, sought holiness and righteousness and separated themselves unto God. The Lord has sent hundreds from around the globe to fellowship and share their labors.

Unbeknown to this band of saints, they purchased land by faith, land with a special blessing on it. Here, they have been blessed by visitations of God's Presence. One night, shortly after their establishment, a neighboring pastor came to worship with them. Not accustomed to their ways, he excused himself after the meeting and, with his wife and daughter, drove away. Since it was nightfall, and in the Winter, the air was chilly, enhancing sound. Abrasive sounds were heard from a car speeding backward. Within a few moments, the auto halted about where it was originally parked, but this time a screaming driver cried out, "Look, the fiery cloud, the huge red fiery cloud—it will not let me pass." Those in the main house were already seeing a presence of rolling fire and lights which were so glorious, they defied description. The other occupants of the car were on the ground, praying and trembling. Those inside the house saw this manifestation go up-

96

ward for a short time and settle over a field of blueberries near them. There it remained for about an hour with lightening-like extensions and bright lights focusing on first this section of property, then another. Everyone was trembling and worshipping. (A tape recorder left running, recorded many of the outbursts and reactions of those who had run outside.) The local newspaper reported bright lights hovering to the east of the observer.

After this initial experience, there were many similar evidences, like "portals of Glory" over this group. (In Bible times, there are recorded such portals. Bethel was a portal for Jacob with "angels ascending and descending.")[2]

Enclaves have the burden and blessing of being involved in "awesome deeds of righteousness." Loosing angels, acting as connective links to others engaged in God's works, sending emissaries beyond their locales to others and to other nations—to speak words of the Lord over individuals, areas, cities and countries, this is their labor.

The Arkansas group goes beyond requirements and educates their children in Hebrew and Greek as well as two other languages, following a rigid curriculum. They introduce their youth to spiritual matters, encouraging them in the gifts of the Spirit. Their calling is not to endogamy, but equipage. Herein lies the fault of many community efforts, the outward visage often takes a back seat to self-ministry.

Enclaves should have the same qualifications as the seven thousand of Elijah's time, not bowing the knee or expressing affection for that which man regales, but being the possession of the Lord. There is a difference!

How many of these individuals and groups are in the earth? Perhaps like Elijah and Elisha, they have an appointed day to meet, but today are unaware of the other's presence. Each setting is strategically molded to be what the Lord needs them to be for special and specific tasks.

Those who are ranked symbolically as the "the present day seven thousand," find themselves being changed inwardly. Recently, a warrior who resides in Minnesota was heard to say, "I asked God to shake loose all that which was shakable in the earth and leave that which was unshakable—little did I realize He would begin with me. Such prayer has led me to wonder if I am the only one alive who seeks to live every moment unto Him." Warrior, be introduced to Elijah!

CHAPTER SEVEN

Holy Is

> For I am the LORD your God. You shall
> therefore consecrate yourselves,
> and you shall be holy; for I am holy.
> Leviticus 11:44 (NKJV)

(Leaving the combination of holiness and righteousness, it is time to turn attention to the words: holy and righteous. They form a somewhat different study, even though connected to their cousins.)

Holy, the Adjective

"Holy" cannot be defined apart from holiness. Great confusion arises when people attempt to separate the adjective, holy, from the noun, holiness. Holy is the extension of what is known as Holiness-Being; holy, then, is the <u>only</u> descriptor which can be used for the actions or expressions of a Holiness-Being.

When God appeared in the burning bush, Moses found himself standing on "holy" ground. The dirt beneath Moses was not in itself "holy," but when the Lord was present—His holiness extended to the earth around Moses.

Herein lies the reason for study in this chapter: Man has attempted to assign "holy" to that which is not connected intimately to Holiness-Being. Objects, places, works and people are often described as "holy," when, in reality, they may not be extensions and expressions of Holiness at all. In tracing the word, Holy, through scripture, one observes some peculiarities associated with the term.

Definition

Exodus is the first book to begin using the adjective, "holy," and from the moment it was first used to the present day, man has had to assess what is holy and what is not. *Qadosh* (holy) is used early in Exodus (19:6), and there it revealed its truest form—as an expression of relationship.

> 'And you shall be unto me a kingdom of priests, and a holy nation.' (NKJV)

"Obey my voice," precedes this most intimate of pleas. According to this passage, a "holy nation" is dependent on an intimate relation to a Holy God. "Me," a possessive pronoun, conveys a desire to bring one into favor. The "You-Me" construct destroys an "I-Thou" theology.

Isaiah 58:13-14 reiterates this truth:

> If you turn away thy foot from the Sabbath, from doing thy pleasure on my holy day; and call the Sabbath a delight, the holy of the Lord, honorable; and shalt honor him, not doing thine own ways, nor finding thine own pleasure, nor speaking thine own words: Then shalt thou delight thyself in the Lord. (NKJV)

Inevitably, through the sieve of the mind, man heard "Priests" and "Sabbath," while failing to hear: "unto Me" and "nor speaking thine own words." Priests appeared who spoke their own words, and subsequently, "sacred" took the place of holy. Man has a way of devoting things to God rather than devoting himself or herself to Him. Men relish the office of Priest and the exalted office of High Priest more than the ministry accompanying it. Clerics were more interested in establishing rules about the Sabbath and how to keep them, than delighting in their relationship with the God of the Sabbath. Most of them had no relation to delight in. "Holy man" became a desired title, more than an adjective describing the character of the servant. "Holy" began to take character apart from its servile position as a descriptor, but "holy" has no existence without holiness.

"Holy" is an adjective in Scripture, an adjective which is applied to deeds, objects, places and some people (those who are members of the family of holiness). Just as God is holy, His people must be holy—in exactly the same manner. Holiness is founded in God's innermost person. Holiness, which emanates from within God, must also emanate from within man.

"Holy" is a state of being, for one simply is or one is not—holy. Similar in form to the old physician's cliché, "No female is just a little pregnant; she is or is not." A person is either holy or not.

Far too long, the church and the world have jointly classified situations, items and people as holy, when, in reality, they were not. Ranging from Hindu Temples and Islamic Mosques to Cathedrals and "churches in the Wildwood," the list of "holy" places grows in proportion to the distortion of truth. Designations of "holy," by a religious populace long divorced from the Most High Holy One (Isaiah 40:25), has proven the need to find God's definition of the term.

Holy versus the Sacred

Definition is found in His Name. His Name is the starting place for defining the term. Where His Name dwells is "the holy" place, and the people who dwell with him are contrite and humble and holy.

> For thus says the High and Lofty One, who inhabits eternity, whose **Name is Holy**: 'I dwell in the high and holy place, with him who has a contrite and humble spirit,…'
>
> Isaiah 57:15a (NKJV)

Linkage is extremely important, for every designation of "holy" flows from His Presence.

Vessels, utensils and grails have been deemed "holy" because of their association as instruments of religious service and sacred use. They are only holy because of Him, if holy at all. Nothing is holy when separated from Him. David proved the accuracy of this premise by his actions.

David ate shew bread from sacred pans, and he erected a tabernacle apart from the "holy priests." God saw it and declared He would, "raise the tabernacle of David" in the last days. It is not the "setting apart" that makes an item "holy," rather it is who sanctifies it that makes it "holy."

It is not the symbolism of a cross, a book, an altar or a pew that makes it "holy." It is the presence of God in man or the true believer's own presence that makes anything holy. Jesus "cleansed" a Temple already declared to be "Holy." Not a person present would have agreed that this "holy" place even needed His cleansing. (Such is the difference between the mind of God and the mind of man.)

His act predicated a great truth, which is someone must rise up in the kingdom of God and declare by the Spirit what is truly "holy" and what is not. There must be a cleansing today in the multiple landmarks dedicated to God as "holy."

When Holiness departs, Holy departs also. Only when the designated place or thing relates to His holiness can it bear the adjective: " Holy." (Bethel was Holy because the presence of God was there, and it carried that uniqueness in Jacob [Israel]'s heart.)

It is a "holy" Temple when the Lord is present. It is a "holy" altar when God **accepts** sacrifices or prayers from it. Petitions are "holy" when offered by a people of holiness. Where He is, there is the 'Holy.'

Holy is where He dwells. For instance, He dwells in His "holy" mountain. Although different, the mountain Moses approached was "holy" because God came there. One may find him or herself praying in a "holy" closet, living in a "holy" house, surrounded by "holy" people, as long as the true criteria for the adjective "holy" is met. Holy is an extension of His Holiness, and it is the same with man.

Common Error

Vine was completely correct when he declared:

> The traditional understanding of "holy" as meaning "separated" is only a <u>derived</u> meaning, and not the primary.[1]

Vine's observation about "derived" meaning is more than significant; it is a modifying correction to dozens of doctrinal statements which have strayed from truth.

One of the great tragedies in Christendom has been the use of this derived meaning, rather than the primary one. Confused with various doctrines of sanctification misapplied to cultural symbols and detached from the Holiness-Presence of God, whole theologies have risen to present false hope and to create an illusion of the holy. Congregations have been told, "You are a royal priesthood and a holy people;" wholesalely, when in reality, those congregations have never known or experienced the presence of the Lord and haven't the foggiest concept of what "holy" means.

Ministers and priests have created more illusion than the craftiest of magicians by creating their illusions around self-determined definitions of "holy," all the while divorcing it from holiness. Their delusions have swept through denominations and fellowships to the ruin of their constituents. Great numbers of congregants have never experienced what God has designed for those who are truly "Holy," because they have been denied God's definition. To keep a steady stream of Bible Study that does not inculcate truth about the "holy," is to develop a people with historical knowledge, while being devoid of spiritual knowledge. Being "holy" in real terms eludes the vast majority of "believers." How can they know "holy," when all they have been shown is a cloistered nun, a saffron-robed priest, a collared clergy or a duped deacon.

Let the first shot be fired over the bow of the ship of religious despotism, for those who know the truth are coming aboard! A defining re-read of the following passage is necessary:

> For thus says the High and Lofty One, who inhabits eternity, whose Name is Holy: 'I dwell in the high and holy place, with him who has a contrite and humble spirit,...'
>
> Isaiah 57:15a (NKJV)

The common denominator in this favored group is the adjective: "Holy!"

A quick review of the multitudes who claim to have religion will reveal their unholy state. Sanctimony has replaced being sanctified (the state of Holiness Being). "Sanctified" has placated the "holy" in the religious mind. Sanctification has become a doctrinal assurance associated with whatever cultural formula any given religious institution might contrive. Sanctification varies by man's definition and has no status in the living God.

Sanctification and the Holy

Sanctification (hagios) is the Greek word found in the New Testament which is **most** associated with the term HOLY. Doctrines of sanctification range from being "appropriated" to all saints (at the moment of their salvation), all the way across the compendium to mean: "arriving at spiritual maturity." One is fiat, the other evolutionary.

Sanctification, though, began in the Old Testament as a precursor of "holy." It began its existence in Exodus and had to do with "severing oneself from every connection but God!" It called for more than a separation "unto;" it promoted an "overtaking of" the wealth of blessing flowing from the Lord (found only in Holiness-Being).

Sanctification once was the major ingredient in setting one's life to align with holiness in order to be holy before the judgments of God. To be sanctified was the most important of pursuits. To stand as "holy" before a Holy God was the ultimate goal for life. This must still be the case because the Lord is coming in these last days and bringing His judgment with Him. (Away with doctrinal statements and treatises! Let "holy" characterize God's people, places and things.)

New Testament Views of Old Testament Ways

Holy is the pervasive link between the Old Testament and the New. Its derivations and nuances do not change from Genesis to Revelation. In the Old Testament, the emphasis was on being Holy men of God.

In the New Testament, the subject matter is similarly of "holy men of God:"

> For He received from God the Father honor
> and glory when such a voice came to Him from
> the Excellent Glory: 'This is My beloved Son,

in whom I am well pleased.' And we heard this voice which came from heaven when we were with Him on the <u>holy</u> mountain. And so we have the prophetic word confirmed, which you do well to heed as a light that shines in a dark place, until the day dawns and the morning star rises in your hearts; knowing this first, that no prophecy of Scripture is of any private interpretation, for prophecy never came by the will of man, but <u>holy</u> men of God spoke as they were moved by the <u>Holy</u> Spirit.

2 Peter 1:17-21 (NKJV)

Every element of this verse screams relationship. The mountain was "holy" because He was present. The men were "holy" because they were "of God." The Holy Spirit is Holy because He is God.

If one studies all the passages in Scripture which use the word "holy," an interesting integrant begins to surface. Holy is primarily associated with God, the places He dwells, the things He designates as holy and the people He communes with.

Intense study will produce another essential—the lack of degrees of holy. Again, using the "expectant mother example," one may exclaim, upon observation of the woman's mid-section, "she is really pregnant!" What one is observing is a twofold manifestation: the advanced term and the evident fact. Both these concepts are applicable to the word, "holy." Evidences of "holy" may be more apparent on some occasions than others, but "holy" IS.

Spiritual Solutions

Deeply involved in what is described as "holy" is the companion affirmation of righteous. When the Holy One extends His love toward His children or to a sinner, righteousness

106

(dwelling within Him) determines or judges the act as "righteous" and declares: "That is holy." In the millisecond when Holiness issues love out of His inner being, righteousness (which has built into His nature to pronounce judgment) MUST declare: HOLY! The Regal Pair are coterminous.

When Compassion was poured forth, when Healing was called into being, when Forgiveness was issued, when Encouragement was given, when Creation was accomplished, all of them had simultaneous responses from righteousness: He pronounced them "HOLY."

Deep inside the true believer, when holiness bears its fruit and the soul reaches forth to produce what the epistles call for (and the example of Jesus reveals)—in that moment—righteousness affirms: It is "holy!" The foundation of all acceptable action for the believer is holiness and righteousness. Love becomes an expression of Holiness, so does wrath.

Herein lies the answer to man's struggle with the wrath of God. Some may question how a Holy God could create hell (Luke 16:19-31 emphasis on 31), rain down judgment on a city or nation (Genesis19, Sodom and Egypt, Exodus 12:29), extend His reach to destroy a person (Er and Onan in Genesis 38:7,10 ; Nadab and Abihu, Leviticus 10:1-3), or give command to take away land occupied by one people in order to give it to another (Numbers 33:50-56). The dilemma is solved when one views these matters as acts established in holiness and emanating from holiness. They are holy.

The same principle is true whenever God issues forth His wrath—righteousness takes notice and pronounces it, "Holy!" Connected to each of the cited examples, a closer examination will reveal some form of "profaneness" associated with each incidence. This is why Holiness released wrath. Nadab and Abihu offered "profane" fire, and God's Holiness released wrath. (Holiness will not abide "profaneness," and whatever

107

corrective force is required to confront or eradicate it—is immediate and declared, "holy.")

Jesus understood this relationship. His total ministry was the extension of Holiness, either in love or in wrath. He had compassion on the multitudes, forgave their sins, healed their sick. He moved among them as a teacher explaining the closeness of heaven to earth. They had forgotten how involved God had been with man in earlier generations. They lost sight of the "holy" assignation of God as well.

> '...By those who come near Me, I must be re-
> garded as holy; and before all the people, I
> must be glorified.'   Leviticus 10:3 NKJV)

The same arm, who reached to pull the lame man to his feet, grasped the thongs of a whip and entered the Temple. Both acts were "holy" in the sight of Righteousness and the Father. The mouth that spoke healing to whole villages, also condemned wholesalely—the Scribes and Pharisees. Yet, He was holy in all His work. When the early disciples prayed in Acts 4:30, they did so in the Name of "Your holy Servant, Jesus." Jesus, the Great High Priest, separated the holy from the profane and taught the people the difference. He did so with one resounding commentary, "The kingdom of heaven IS AT HAND." He executed the office of the Great High Priest, fulfilling both Ezekiel and Hebrews (meeting the requirements of both Old and New Testaments).

The Work of a True Priesthood

Distinguishing the holy from the profane was the primary duty of the priests in the time of Moses (Leviticus 10:10). What happened in the millenniums between Moses' instructions to the priesthood and the arrival of the Great High Priest, Jesus? Spiritual erosion of the term "Holy" is what happened. God's expectations were always the same, but their interpretation led them astray.

How different is this today? None! Definition by the modern fivefold ministry does not include bringing people to holiness and teaching them the difference between the clean and the unclean—the holy and profane. Defenders say that the fivefold ministry is more complicated today than then. However difficult a job description for these offices may be in the Twenty-first Century, duty is duty. The Old Testament priests somehow lost their perspective of holiness and therefore lost their mission, so when Jesus arrived—nothing resembled their initial mandate. This is the dilemma today! One wonders: "Will this be the case when He comes again?"

Teaching people the difference between the holy and the profane was tantamount to priestly duty, and Jesus sought to restore that cause, not in the established Temple, but in His newly founded body. In the Twenty-first Century, the task is even more daunting, due in part to the proliferation of error regarding the definition of "holy." What are the results of these errors?

First and foremost is an almost universal disbelief that God is actively involved in the intricate affairs of man. No one expects Ananias and Sapphira to die in his or her midst because no one believes the Holy Spirit can be "lied to" in modern parlance. In similarity, few believe the "kingdom of God is truly at hand." There are no blind Elymus's wandering about under the corrective hand of a "holy" Paul.

When the profane one reached for the prophet Jeremiah, a shriveled arm was drawn back; when the profane congregation reaches toward God, a shriveled church draws back.

Ezekiel 44 addressed the heart of the issue. The people of Ezekiel's day were ignorant of the difference between the holy and the profane. Consequently, they tolerated the intolerable in their clergy and their religious affairs. Today, the same scenario is in place. Ezekiel's bunch worshipped according to the dictates of the custom of the day and that custom was rife with spiritual pollution. Their punishment was simple: God departed from their midst. A remnant was positioned, however; they were the Sons of Zadok. They had kept the holy from the profane and sought to teach the people the difference; therefore, God was available to the Zadok priesthood. Their name meant "righteous," and they were also holy.

What did they teach the people? What did they feel was primary to their "keeping 'that which remained' alive?" First, they made sure their worship was pure, their lives were pure and their demeanor among the people was holy. THEN, they were instructed in how to teach the people the difference between the holy and the profane, the clean and the unclean.

> 'In controversy they shall stand as judges, and judge it according to My judgments. They shall keep My laws and My statutes in all My appointed meetings and they shall hallow My Sabbaths.'   Ezekiel 44:24 (NKJV)

They had to call things as God called them (letting righteousness and the Spirit determine the holy). They had to keep His commands in all their appointed meetings (Emphasis on this aspect of Holiness can be found in Romans 1:4; Romans 7:12). They had to make holy the Sabbaths (the day consecrated out of seven). Ezekiel used the Zadok priesthood as an example of what true priesthood is. If God's people are to be priests, they must follow this example. The New Testament writers never lost sight of the true priesthood.

Holy Glory

Paul taught, in Romans 11:16, that Gentiles were grafted in to redemption because of the holy judgment of God. God broke off the unholy in order to establish the holy.

> For if the firstfruit is holy, the lump is also
> holy; and if the root is holy, so are the branches.
>
> (NKJV)

Then Paul declared a message rarely heard in preaching circles Romans 11:231-22 (NKJV):

> For if God did not spare the natural branches,
> <u>He may not spare you either (a message which
> will occupy few, if any, pulpits next Sunday)</u>.
> Therefore consider the goodness and severity
> of God: on those who fell severity; but toward
> you goodness. <u>Otherwise you also will be cut
> off</u>.

"Holy" is on the cutting edge of the judgments of God. Holiness pleases God; Holy describes all with which He associates. Knowing this, Paul insisted the body be the "holy" temple (with which "holy" hands are raised and "holy" kisses administered); he could not conceive of the "unholy" church which exists today.

> that He might present it to Himself a <u>glorious</u>
> church, not having spot or wrinkle or any such
> thing, but that it should be HOLY and without
> blemish.   Ephesians 5:27 (NKJV)

Holy Glory

Holy Glory cannot fall on an unholy body; for a church to be glorious, it must be filled with "Holy Glory."

It is Holy glory that is called for, not the glorying of one's occasions in worship and praise, but that which is born out of humility and contriteness—His Presence.

Again in Colossians 1:21ff Paul affirms:

> And you, who once were alienated and en-
> emies in your mind by wicked works, yet now
> He has reconciled in the body of His flesh

111

through death, to present you HOLY, and blameless and **irreproachable** in His sight — **IF** indeed you continue in the faith, grounded and steadfast are not moved away from the gospel.   (NKJV)

If one wishes to examine the true apostles creed, examine how much of their writing concentrated on the "holy." Simon Peter and Jude spent a greater percentage of their writing emphasizing the "holy," more than on any other subject. They were in league with Revelation which dedicated all the end-time blessings to the "holy."

The church can no longer sustain itself before God and His word and remain in ignorance of the difference between the holy and the profane. Holy IS!

CHAPTER EIGHT

Something Is Missing
In The Temple

> All the people shouted with a great shout,
> when they praised the Lord, because
> the foundation of the house of the Lord was laid. But
> many of the priests and Levites and heads
> of the fathers' houses, who were old men,
> who had seen the first temple,
> wept with a loud voice...
> Ezra 3:11b,12a (NKJV)

Missing Elements

Jews unanimously acknowledge that five things were want
ing in the second temple which were found in the first,
namely:

1. The ark;
2. The holy spirit of prophecy;
3. The Urim and Thummim;
4. The sacred fire; (that came down from heaven)
5. The Shekinah. (Presence of God) [1]

Such an acknowledgement was an acquiescence on their

part to two important axioms: First, the lack of these five elements posed no impediment in their ability to continue religious activities in an under-powered Temple; second, the elements were deemed non-essential to Temple praise and worship. In other words, they were willing to accept the second Temple as a "substitute" Temple to replace the original "holy" Temple.

Jewish leadership decided the substitute Temple would be accepted as the legitimate Temple in which they would invest their lives, even though it had shortages. Secondly, they reckoned the absence of the five elements as an inevitable loss because of the captivity. For them to continue in the second Temple, they were obliged to accept the second-rate character of it. In another light, they reasoned "it was the best they could hope for under the circumstances."

Thousands worship in similar surroundings every week. Whether it be a congregational gathering (cathedral, church, home fellowship) or in the temple of the inner man, they know something is missing in their temple. Most have acquiesced in some fashion or other to approve the "substitute" rather than reach for the Holy.

A problem exists with this kind of reasoning. In order for the second Temple to qualify as a "Holy" Temple (the place where God met man and true worship took place), the missing five parts would have to be restored and their place acknowledged as essential.

The missing parts were the integral ingredients for being qualified as "holy." Reviewing the progressive value-loss of each missing part will cause one to re-assess its place of honor.

The Ark

Starting with the loss of the ark, as one looks above and in it, its integral value mounts. This was where the supreme blood sacrifice was laid, and thereby, no altar meant no acceptable sacrifice. Another reason the substitute Temple could not suffice is it would require placing a false representation of the real (since the real ark was gone) in the holiest of places. A laver for blood and two cherubim would never find rest on a substitute ark.

Inside the original ark, which was designed and required by God to be placed in the most holy place, were articles of His manifest work: the budding rod, the manna of the wilderness (in a golden pot) and the Tablets (ten commandments). These God-required items were also missing. They were not symbols; they were not museum pieces to be treasured from generation to generation and gazed upon as mere tangibles of a past civilization—these were articles designed by, touched by, and which bore the testimony of God's power and Holiness.

The Budding Rod/ Manna/Tablets

Aaron's budding rod was indicative of resurrection power; the manna in a golden container represented the bread of the living word; the tablets of stone were the covenant of the Law, the fulfillment of God's promise. (All these elements were present in the womb of Mary and found completion in Jesus' life.) When one considers the absence of the ark in the second Temple and considers the spiritual deprivation its absence brought, is it any wonder the elders wept while beholding the new structure?

If, however, the ark had been the only absent part in the second Temple, it alone would have robbed this "Center of Worship" of its characterization as "holy;" nevertheless, it was joined by four other elements.

Holy Spirit of Prophecy

The holy spirit of prophesy was also absent. The Spirit of prophesy was God's method of communication through

115

"holy men of God (a characterization not limited to those who were named in the word of God or to those like Isaiah or Jeremiah, who have authored books)." God's prophetic message was not heard in the Temple again. Warnings, blessings, God's fresh words about past, present or future happenings were missing from the scene. Suffering the absence of this ingredient alone should have amounted to a loss greater than the populace would bear, but still other items were added to the list.

Urim and Thummim

Urim and Thummim, the lights and perfections of Godly wisdom and direction, were the third missing ingredient. Present in the first Temple and worn as part of the High Priest's breastplate, they offered the visionary interaction between heaven and earth. Their absence caused a Herculean vacuum. Jews, since the time of Moses, respected the unique place Urim and Thummim occupied in the Tabernacle and Temple, acknowledging their supernatural origin (not derived from man's hands).

> Rabbi Menachem said, "The Urim and Thummim were not the work of the artificer; neither had the artificers or the congregation of Israel in them any work or any voluntary offering, but they were a mystery delivered to Moses from the mouth of God, or they were the work of God himself, or a measure of the Holy Spirit."[2]

The Scripture was explicit about who was responsible to them and how they would be worn:

> 'So Aaron shall bear the names of the sons of Israel on the breastplate of judgment over his heart, when he goes into the holy place, as a

memorial before the LORD continually. And
you shall put in the breastplate of judgment
the Urim and the Thummim, and they shall be
over Aaron's heart when he goes in before the
LORD. So Aaron shall bear the judgment of
the children of Israel over his heart before the
LORD continually.'

Exodus 28:29-30 (NKJV)

'Let Your Thummim and Your Urim be with
Your holy one.'

Deuteronomy 33:8 (NKJV)

Early in the progress toward building this second Temple,
leadership fully expected that Urim and Thummim would be
regained for the priestly use, but this was not the case.

And the governor said to them that they should
not eat of the most holy things till a priest could
consult with the Urim and Thummim.

Ezra 2:63 (NKJV)

(The governor's expectancy was evident in this passage,
but the elements never arrived.)

How could those meeting in the second Temple function
without God's wisdom and knowledge flowing into them and
giving them direction? David often consulted whether to enter battle or not through this method; the Holy Ghost would
move on the priest as he beheld the breastplate, and there he
saw the vision of prophecy (Numbers 27:18,21; Judges 1:1;
20:18,28; 1 Sam 23:9-12; 28:6). With the vision came the
insight, for Urim and Thummim linked heaven and earth in
real time. The loss of such input caused the Temple to lose
one of its strongest drawing forces—supernatural consulta-
tion for the affairs of life.

Urim and Thummim's loss was tantamount to the "heavenly lights being shut off."

Since the word 'uwriym signifies "LIGHTS," and the word thumiym, "PERFECTIONS," they were probably designed to point out the light—the abundant information, in spiritual things, afforded by the wonderful revelation which God made of himself by and under the LAW; and the perfection—**entire holiness** and strict conformity to Himself, which this dispensation required, and which are introduced and accomplished by that dispensation of light and truth, the GOSPEL, which was prefigured and pointed out by the law and its sacrifices. [3]

Under the theocracy of God, the loss of Lights and Perfections emphasized the fact that God was not present. Up to the time of their departure, the high priest's ability to know the mind of the Lord depended solely on the functioning of the Urim and Thummim.

He (the priest) shall be endued with a power of knowing and making known the mind of God in all difficult doubtful cases, relating either to the civil or ecclesiastical state of the nation. Their (Israeli) government was a theocracy: God was their King, the high priest was, under God, their ruler, the Urim and Thummim were his cabinet-council.[4]

No longer could they wield that "special understanding," so necessary in making eternal, as well as, everyday decisions. Those who were directed about in a wilderness with cloud and fire and had been enlightened by Urim and Thummim to guide their lives in the promised land suddenly were destined to "go it alone." The result was four hundred years of Rabbinic definition and redefinition, leading to the morass encountered by Jesus.

If this, however, was the end of their loss, its sum would have been decimating enough—but there was more. The sacred fire was missing.

The Sacred Fire

Two of the most momentous times in history were marked by the fire of God falling upon the altar of sacrifice.

Under Moses:

> And Moses and Aaron went into the tabernacle of meeting, and came out and blessed the people. Then the glory of the LORD appeared to all the people, and fire came out from before the LORD and consumed the burnt offering and the fat on the altar. When all the people saw it, they shouted and fell on their faces.
>
> Leviticus 9:23-24 (NKJV)

Under Solomon:

> When Solomon finished praying, fire came down from heaven and consumed the burnt offering and the sacrifices, and the glory of the LORD filled the temple. The priests could not enter the temple of the LORD because the glory of the LORD filled it. When all the Israelites saw the fire coming down and the glory of the LORD above the temple, they knelt on the pavement with their faces to the ground, and they worshiped and gave thanks to the LORD, saying, 'He is good; and his love endures forever.'
>
> 2 Chronicles 7:1-3 (NIV)

In both these passages, the falling of the fire and the Presence of the Lord were synchronized. They were connected; so was their absence.

When the second Temple was inaugurated, no such fire fell upon the altar, no Presence (glory) appeared. Though there was rejoicing by one group at the raising up of the Temple, there was weeping by an older group who were sorrowful for the loss.

Combined, these five elements represented every aspect of approval and license for Temple operation. When the remnant dedicated the new structure, vivid contrast was shown between what was separated unto God by man and what was deemed "holy" by God. It isn't "holy," until He says it's "holy." Ensuing years, without the ark, the Holy Spirit of prophesy, Urim and Thummim, the sacred fire and the glory Presence of God, led to compromise and entrenched legalism. Moses would have been astonished at the resulting loss, even though he prophesied about it darkly. Instead, Jesus was outraged!

If historical precedence means anything, its graphics produce a backdrop for modern appraisal. The church of today functions like the second Temple, without the elements it needs for spiritual license to operate.

Discovering the Five Elements in the Early Church

Resurrection power brought the original church into being. The word, fulfilled through Jesus, and prophesy came together and formed its roots. A new covenant in the blood of Jesus forged its message.

Armed with the "gospel of the kingdom," the disciples touched the lives of the ancient world. All the elements missing in the Temple were discovered in the early church. The Holy Spirit of prophesy wrote through Matthew, Mark, Luke, John, Paul and reveled in John's Revelation. Urim and Thummim was present in the believer's breast plate of righteousness. The Holy Spirit directed, guided and taught unlearned men with such consistency they dared not venture without hearing from Him. Cloven tongues of Fire and Glory came down upon those gathered in the appointed Holiest of Holies (upper room). The assembled inward temples formed a greater Temple than Moses.' Individually, as Priests, standing at the throne of God with boldness, they superceded the Levites of yesteryear. Miracles, supernatural meetings, powerful advances in conversion and Spirit anointing became the norm. In comparison and contrast to the Second Temple, where they once worshipped, there was no contest (Not only was there fluidity among them, there was also freedom.)

Soon, each convert discovered that which was missing in the stone and mortar Temple was present in the Temple of his or her heart. They worshipped God just as Jesus had prophesied to the Samaritan woman—not in Samaria or Jerusalem, but in the Spirit and truth of their inner person. Able to pray without positioning, consult without schedule, convene without appointment—the early church lived in the Presence of God.

Not so Today! Trekking through two millenniums, most congregations, as well as individuals, have suffered similar losses to the second Temple. Worship is attempted without the fire and presence of God. Life decisions are determined without the Holy Spirit. Prophesy has turned into a tool of the mind and heart of man, rather than speaking sovereign words heard from the Holy Temple.

Missing in the Modern Church

Divested of holiness and operating without license, the tragic results are the same as the second Temple: A multitude believing that "all is well"—to the outrage of the Trinity. No longer a holy communion engaged by holy people, the empty shell of church and man ritualistically performs "sacred" duties without repentance. No effort is made to re-establish the lost elements the early church prized so greatly. The lights and perfections are no longer in place in lives or congregations, but no one is aware of their absence. Multitudes were not aware at the second Temple; they are not aware today!

How did this sad state come to be? Moses warned those entering the promised land when he exposed the root of all spiritual problems as being presumption (pride and arrogance: Deuteronomy 17:12 and18:22; Psalms 13:10). In their fullness of riches and pride, man's reasoning replaced the contrite holiness necessary to function under the blessings of God.

Jesus attacked similar problems in the second Temple. He began with the Temple leadership and pointed out their presumptiveness in dealing with the issue of oaths. In Matthew 23:16, after a railing castigation against the scribes and Pharisees, peeling back their hypocrisy and exposing their shameless pride, He connected the substitute Temple to their personal substitute holiness. Their extortion and self-indulgence had led them to a place where every smidgeon of holiness was wrung from their worship.

> Woe to you, blind guides, who say, 'Whoever swears by the temple, it is nothing; but whoever swears by the gold of the temple, he is obliged to perform it.' Fools and blind! For which is greater, the gold or the temple that sanctifies the gold? And, "Whoever swears by the altar, it is nothing; but whoever swears by the gift that is on it, he is obliged to perform it." Fools and blind! For which is greater, the gift or the altar that sanctifies the gift? Therefore he who swears by the altar, swears by it and by all things on it. He who swears by the temple, swears by it and by Him who dwells in it. And he who swears by heaven, swears by the throne of God and by Him who sits on

it. Woe to you, scribes and Pharisees, hypocrites! For you pay <u>tithe of mint and anise and
cummin</u>, and have neglected the weightier
matters of the law: justice and mercy and faith.
These you ought to have done, without leaving the others undone.

Matthew 23:16-23 (NKJV)

By taking the leadership to task over one of their many
rules, Jesus contrasted their mockery to the true holiness which
He associated with the real Temple. He looked at the Second
Temple and contrasted it to the Heavenly Temple, just as
Ezekiel did in the latter chapters of his prophesy. Every underlined word in the above passage is what man contributed
to the Temple, and every detail Jesus points to is one sanctified by the Lord in holiness. A gift on an "unholy" altar is
declared "unholy." Herein is the difficulty modern Christianity has with tithing and "promises of the hundred and thousand fold blessing," it is the altar—not the gift—that sanctifies. The gilding on the edifice does not create holiness; it
simply shows the art of man in the same manner huge centers
of worship unfurl the banner of wealth on the flagpole of ego.

> The temple and altar were dedicated to God
> fixedly, the gold and gift but secondarily. Christ
> is our altar (Hebrews 13:10), our temple (John
> 2:21); for it is he that sanctifies all our gifts,
> and puts an acceptableness in them, 1 Peter
> 2:5. Those that put their own works into the
> place of Christ's righteousness in justification
> are guilty of the Pharisees' absurdity, who pre-
> ferred the gift before the altar. <u>Every true Chris-
> tian is a living temple</u>; and by virtue thereof
> common things are sanctified to him; 'unto
> the pure all things are pure...'   Titus 1:15 [5]

Neither gift nor gold meant anything to Jesus, who looked highly upon the widow's mite. To Him, the character of the Temple was to be drawn from its regard to holiness and righteousness. Temple character was determined by the "holiness" of the altar, which related to the fear and reverence shown to the God of that Temple. One simple rule was given to Moses, by that same God, immediately following the burning of Nadab and Abihu, who offered an unacceptable offering in "golden censers" before the Lord:

> By those who come near Me I must be regarded
> as HOLY And before all the people I must be
> glorified.   Leviticus 10:3 (NKJV)

A common error pervades Christendom: Those who enter the gates of worship have forgotten Leviticus 10:3. Even in the inner-sanctum of the heart, the holiness of the God we address is often lost in flippant rhetoric. When hearts assembled in the first Temple, the gravity of fire and smoke caused them to glorify God and regard Him as Holy.

Similar Circumstances

Twenty-first Century worshippers have yet to experience the power of such assemblage—where holy people gather in holiness before the God of holiness and worship him in the beauty of holiness. Without the gathering of those who have the common experience of communion in the Holy Spirit joining together in holiness, the world has yet to behold the "church."

The Temple of the Inward Man

Long before such a gathering takes place, there must be a cleansing of the Temple of the heart and the establishment of all the holy essentials (the installation of the five missing parts mentioned above). There cannot just be "the living Word;" there must also be resurrection life, covenant fulfillment, lights and perfections, holy fire and the Presence of God. The believer does not approach a stolid idol, but an unlimited holy Majesty!

Paul spoke repeatedly about the "inner man of the heart" and emphasized that "ye are the Temple of the Holy Spirit." It was Paul who flatly declared that anyone who defiles the Body-Temple, "God will Destroy." Is it not strange, in all the preaching, teaching, prophesying and conferencing done among Christian people, this passage is NEVER chosen to be the topic for a message?

> Now if anyone builds on this foundation with gold, silver, precious stones, wood, hay, straw, each one's work will become clear; for the Day will declare it, because it will be revealed by fire; and the fire will test each one's work, of what sort it is. If anyone's work which he has built on it endures, he will receive a reward. If anyone's work is burned, he will suffer loss; but he himself will be saved, yet so as through fire. Do you <u>not know that **you** are the temple of God and that the Spirit of God dwells in you</u>? If anyone defiles the temple of God, **God will destroy him**. <u>For the temple of God is holy, which temple you are.</u>
>
> 1 Corinthians 3:12-17 (NKJV)

Divine worship goes on in the inner Temple; it is here the tithe offering or gift is first laid (long before it is laid on man's table or placed in an offering plate). It is here sin is laid bare and exposed and cleansed by the blood. It is here that prayers of intercession are made before the very throne of God, and the incense of holiness is mingled with them. It is here that wisdom is requested and granted. Here, the Holy Spirit directs the proper language, the cadence of delivery and the timing of each offering and request. Here, His conviction is drawn upon. Long before knees touch the floor, there is a spreading forth of one's spirit-frame lying prostrate before His Holiness. "Holy" is the word breathed from one's lips in the wake of all other considerations of heaven and earth. Silence often prevails, as words seem like babble, and thoughts not captured are being gathered to lay at His feet. This is the Holy Temple that Jesus spoke to the woman about while His disciples were having unholy thoughts. This is the temple where the Holy Spirit dwells and leads a worship service of indescribable tenor. Honesty prevails and truth is the only appropriate word.

Garments of the body are insignificant here, for no flesh glories before Him. The amount of giving and the flare of recognition is lost in the eternal spectra of His glory. There arises a sense that angels are present To merely meditate or bring a thought is to minister before an altar overseen by the Great High Priest, Jesus. Ministration is made in such a way as one could never accomplish apart from Him. This is the required premise of true fellowship.

When like-experienced souls join under the leadership of the Spirit in circumstance or location, there is the CHURCH. (Holy within man's inner temple guarantees Holy manifestation outside it. If what comes out of man is holy, he is undefiled.) Modern man is attuned to the sacred more than he is attuned to the holy.

Paul sought to establish a dividing line between those who practiced "the sacred" and those who dwelled in the "Holy." Unbelievers were defined as those who did not worship in the Holy temple of the heart. Believers were defined as those who did.

> Do not be unequally yoked together with unbelievers. For what <u>fellowship</u> has righteousness with lawlessness? And what <u>commun-</u>

126

ion has light with darkness? And what accord has Christ with Belial? Or what part has a believer with an unbeliever? And what agreement has the temple of God with idols? For you are the temple of the living God. As God has said:

'I will dwell in them
And walk among them.
I will be their God,
And they shall be My people.'
Therefore 'Come out from among them
And be separate, says the Lord.
Do not touch what is unclean,
And I will receive you.'
'I will be a Father to you,
And you shall be My sons and daughters,
Says the LORD Almighty.'
2 Corinthians 6:14-18 (NKJV)

Now, following these poignant verses, he caps all of it with this verse:

Therefore, having these promises, beloved, let us cleanse ourselves from all filthiness of the flesh and spirit, *perfecting holiness* in the fear of God.　　　2 Corinthians 7:1 (NKJV)

Such perfecting begins, not in mind-resolve, but in the working of the Spirit in the inner Temple of the heart. Standing in the presence of the Spirit, one is made aware of the "little foxes," and is cleansed of them. Holiness cannot reside alongside unholiness.

Modern Church Versus Early Church

It is in the perfection of holiness which the Twenty-first Century church holds no credentials! Here, precipitous audiences ply social propaganda, manipulated to obliterate the holiness expressed in the former verses. No point of fellowship could ever be established between such an aggregate and the Holiness-believers of the New Testament. Every aspect of what is known as the fellowship of the saints is based on the truth of 2 Corinthians 7:1.

Holiness is the dividing line between all people; Unbelievers and Believers are characterized by their holiness or the lack of it. Deep in the teachings of Paul, this theme arose to confront the Corinthians who lived in a huge metro of debauchery. Homosexuality, prostitution, sexual acts to appease fertility gods and temple sex were paraded on street tile and portico — reviewing this mêlée of filth, there arose the dynamism of Paul's demand for a clean Temple and God's demand for it to be undefiled and holy.

Holy Men In Holy Temples

Holy men of God are the product of worship in a Holy Temple. The earth quakes before them. Nations fear their prospect. One example was John the Baptist, whose holiness caused Kings to quake.

> For Herod feared John, knowing that he was a
> just and **holy** man, and he protected him.
>
> Mark 6:20 (NKJV)

Holy men of God, as in days past, proceeded upon the earth under a different mandate than what is visible among churchmen today. Peter was a fine example: Testifying about the conversion of the Gentiles, he related the angels' visit to Cornelius. The angel, identifying the unknown Simon, said to Cornelius:

> 'Simon whose surname is Peter, who will tell
> you words by which you and all your house-
> hold will be saved.'

128

Then Simon relates how, through this mandate from heaven, the Gentiles received anointing from God:

> 'And <u>as I began to speak, the Holy Spirit</u> fell upon them, as upon us at the beginning.'
>
> Acts 11:12-15 (NKJV)

The underlined passage is testimony enough of the difference between that day and the present one. As Peter began to speak, the Holy Spirit fell on them. Whereas, the wordy ramblings of those bearing the title of "men of God" today have different results than those of Holy Simon.

Lost, to the world of the church today are men so filled with obedience to the Spirit—that they walk into unknown worlds being guided only by the Spirit, speaking holy words to expectant hearts. Lost, to the world of the church are such men who, when they BEGIN to speak, the Holy Spirit falls upon the hearer!

When will holiness begin to reign within the hearts of the people of God so they follow the example of Peter? When will they exult more in the fact their words flow out of the holy temple with Divine results, than that they had opportunity to "speak a few words at the meeting?"

So different was the early disciples' message from modern preaching, that the "established" Twenty-first Century religious leadership feigns to hear it. Their responses are identical to those who chose to cast Paul out for defiling sacred buildings.

> Crying out, "Men of Israel, help! This is the man who teaches all men everywhere against the people, the law, and <u>this place</u>; and furthermore he also brought Greeks into the temple and has defiled this **holy** place.'
>
> Acts 21:28 (NKJV)

The presence of holy men in man's "sacred places" always brings judgment and conviction. It was so with Jesus; it is so today! Something is missing in today's Temples and the likes of Jesus cannot tolerate it! His call for restoration was not the restoration of the Temple, but the restoration of the "Holy" Temple.

> Whom heaven must receive until the **times of restoration** of all things, which God has spoken by the mouth of all His <u>holy prophets</u> since the world began....   Acts 3:21 (NKJV)

The times of Restoration in this passage refer not to the time and place when a worldly church will be instantly changed to a spotless bride. The times of restoration are to be when men are holy and holiness is restored to the heart of all those who live and work in the kingdom.

> Now, therefore, you are no longer strangers and foreigners, but <u>fellow citizens with the saints and members of the household of God</u>, having been built on the foundation of the apostles and prophets, Jesus Christ Himself being the chief cornerstone, in whom the whole building, being joined together, grows into **a holy temple** in the Lord, in whom you also are being built together for **a dwelling place of God in the Spirit**.
>   Ephesians 2:19-22 (NKJV)

CHAPTER NINE

UNHOLY to HOLY:
The Journey

> It is the Christian's duty to force his way into
> the inner circle of saintship.
> Charles H. Spurgeon[1]

Spurgeon did not share a contemporary view of sanctification. He believed that "holy" should be the middle name of all those who claim the name "Christian." His congregants, fellow ministers and correspondents expressed a religious form deemed "unholy" when framed by his Bible. Such error was untenable to him because it was, and is, untenable to God.

Clearly, the New Testament spelled out the intent of the Godhead, to create a fellowship of saints. Three New Testament passages reflect the unity of the Godhead in their work to sanctify (make holy) all those who come to them.

First, Jude (v. 1) opened his letter specifically:

> To those who are called, <u>sanctified by God the Father</u>, and preserved in Jesus Christ.
>
> (NKJV)

Similarly, Paul addressed his Corinthian epistle in this manner:

> To those who are <u>sanctified in Christ Jesus,</u>
> called to be saints
>
> I Corinthians 1:2(NKJV)

Also, Peter qualified his recipients as:

> the) elect according to the foreknowledge of
> God the Father, in <u>sanctification of the Spirit</u>
>
> I Peter 1:2 (NKJV)

Each of these writers exulted in declaring holiness as the chief characteristic of the saints, while addressing definitively the error of those who were not. Jude brilliantly exposed the history of those who refused the offer of the Trinity. He called them, "marked out for condemnation" when they sought to mingle with the redeemed. Jesus called them "tares."

Sowing tares has always been the preferred method of devils. Unbelievers, like those in the ranks of Israel while still in Egypt, were shown to be in league with the disobedient angels formerly of heaven. Sodom and Gomorrah coalesced with "dreamers" who defiled the flesh, rejected authority, and spoke evil of dignitaries. Cain, Balaam and Korah were linked to their modern counterparts who infest love feasts in order to belch their man-modified doctrines. Communing with the lust-filled, the murmurers were exposed as hiding behind sensual crowds. To each of these, Jude cheerfully concluded that the lives of the "saints" stood as a testimony against the hosts of the "unsanctified." (Is it so today?)

Peter resonated as another voice (led by the Spirit) to castigate the unholy by adding the terms "scoffer," "brute beasts" and "the presumptuous" alongside the sermonic catalogue of "great swelling words of emptiness."

Paul joined in the fray by attacking "worldly wisdom"

132

with the same vehemence as he did false prophets— who transform themselves into ministers of righteousness. Paul expounded in the Corinthian letters, "a more perfect way of holiness."

Together, these writers covered all the bases of banality and, in concert, called for the believer to yield his whole being to the masterful work of sanctification (being made holy). In unity, they prioritized their audience as **only** those who were sanctified. Herein lies the leaven of generalizing, as is done in messages which claim promises for the at-large religious community when the promises were given only to the holy people. The promises of God are not made to the unholy.

It is the intent of the God-head to bring a glorious church, without spot or wrinkle, to fullness in the last days—one which is absolutely holy. They co-work to produce a people who are themselves convinced of the high value of holiness (sanctification). Yet, in the Twenty-first Century religious factories, holiness is mostly a concern for those in heaven (as is perfection).

Sanctification, in modern parlance, is no more than a dry doctrine among decaying Theologizers and has found no place at all in the daily walk of those who casually believe. Worldwide, the "religio-moderns" simulate the words of the book of Judges, "they did what is right in their own sight, seeing there was no king."

Christianity has a king, however, who is both "holy" and "undefiled." He is an active king-priest, who has designed a Temple not made with man's hands. He is crafting components without a hammer being heard in the holy city. His work is with His people on the earth. His Temple structure bases everything on the apostles and prophets (holy men) along with Himself as the chief corner stone (the most holy). Living-

Sanctified-Stones are added to the construction, as they conform to His plan. Just as the prophets fit the plan, so did the apostles, and so it must be in this generation.

> He shall build the temple of the Lord: and He
> shall bear the glory.   Zechariah 6:13 (KJV)

Jude, Peter and Paul felt it was not blasphemy to consider themselves equal to, and their ministry coincident with, the patriarchs of the ancient world. Historical holiness has its lineage. Although they were separated by the divide of death, nevertheless, they stood as part of the "cloud of witnesses," joined in synchrony and sanctity alongside the ancients who were made "holy" in Him.

Believers today have been called to this same "holy" lineage, or was there a different "light" for the ancients? Doesn't the same grace that moved in their behalf still operate today? No believer should rest until he or she has equaled Jude, Peter, Paul, John, Moses, Abraham and Noah. They heard from God and did His will. What special dispensation has scripture given for this generation to be less?

As the New Testament writers knew and lived for Jesus and grew to be like Him, did they not set the standard for those who were to follow? Holy heritage is the investment those in the past have made to those of the present and the future. Old world "most holy faith" is no different than New World "most holy faith."

> But you, dear friends, build yourselves up in
> your most holy faith and pray in the Holy
> Spirit.   Jude 20 (NIV)

Just as inter-generational curses (passed down through families) have been exposed and confronted as a force of evil upon the earth, too little has been accredited to blessings that flow forth from inter-generational holiness. Spiritually, the sons and daughters of today benefit from the holy sacrifices and offerings of past saints.

Corporately and individually, "holy" people, in every generation, fellowship inter-generationally with all those who are holy and worship in holiness. Just as the ancients made "holy" sacrifices and gave "holy" offerings, so must modern saints. In so doing, the link of holiness continues unbroken throughout time.

To Aaron, God spoke:

> Here, I Myself have also given you charge of My heave offerings, all the holy gifts of the children of Israel; I have given them as a portion to you and your sons.
>
> Numbers 18:8(NKJV)

In a greater sense, Paul spoke of his work among the Gentiles as a holy offering:

> ...That the offering of the Gentiles might be acceptable, SANCTIFIED by the Holy Spirit.
>
> Romans 15:16 (NKJV)

Holiness has a heritage perpetuated by those yielded to sanctification. "The holy" of all generations share common qualities—they are part of a "holy kingdom."

Biblical standards of holiness (whether Old or New Testament) are not beyond the grasp of the Twenty-first Century believer; indeed, these standards are the only basis for *koinonia* found in the word. Truthfully, the body of believers must confess that their attempts to found their activities apart from the standards of holiness have miserably failed. Those who walk in holiness know there are demands and privileges open to them which are not found in the at-large religious community.

As holy people, fellowship is based not on specious communion or religious preference, for there is no biblical fellowship except among the "holy." Light and darkness are incompatible and the great attempt to ameliorate this by religionists is doomed to despair. Yet, that community (fellowship) based on holiness finds a spiritual bond which cannot be entertained in a worldly church.

Sanctification leads to a perfection unknown and unrealized by the majority who embrace modern theology. Glibly, theologians massage the issue by dividing the subject and speaking of "the perfection of justification" and the "perfection of sanctification." Theologians rightly declare the perfection of justification comes through the perfect substitution of Christ on the cross and the shedding of His blood. Much emphasis is laid on the "imputation of perfection" by Jesus' work, in order for the final perfection to take place in heaven. Philosophically, they dispel any hope of perfection via sanctification while on earth. One must die in order to obtain that perfection which is based on sanctification. According to their reasoning, the believer must spend his or her entire earthly journey without reaching any measure of perfection. Such is man's thinking.

One matter is sure: sanctification (being made holy) begins by teaching the saint not to trust man's reasoning. Grace Roos wrote:

> Being led (by the Spirit) will bring forth some
> strange solutions, some startling revelations...
> as well as train us to cast behind us all the
> natural mind involved.[2]

Being Spirit-determined means putting aside man's mind and reasoning and seeking God's definition and direction.

Spirit-determined living constantly moves toward spiritual perfection. Though the natural mind refuses the thought of any claim to perfection while on earth, such is not foreign to the Spirit. Roos determined that prayer and Bible study were two sides of a perfection triangle, while the third side was closed by Spirit-led maturity. Nothing could be truer! Each is integral to sanctification-perfection. The spotless, unwrinkled Bride will not be imperfect. She is being made perfect through the Spirit. Her final touch of completeness may come on the last hour of the last day, but it will be a final touch, not a beginning touch. Those who leave holiness, righteousness and perfection to heaven need to look at the transmogrify of God's butterfly. Wrapped first as a worm in a cocoon, it is .999 butterfly on its day of breaking loose. One must recognize it is not the responsibility of the saint to judge his state of perfection, only to yield to the Spirit into greater realms of submission and power. The Spirit will make the determination when the finished product is presented. Spirit-determination changes every aspect of "thinking and doing" in the saint's life.

Sanctification (being made holy) changes the aim and direction of its occupant. A saint's aim and action is different from the world, for saints are always conscious of His Presence; they delight in communion with Him. Seeking to know His will, they testify to being citizens of another public. Their actions are different from the "unholy" in that they pursue the right thing even when it harms them. They shun the wrong, even when it would mean a profit or benefit to them. They have no reference point with darkness and reprove those who do. As partakers of the "Divine" nature, they walk in the dignity of such high calling. They protect the lineage of holiness recognized in them and keep it intact and unscathed. Worship, praise, prayer and ponderings bring an awareness of all who have done such in history. Worship, for instance, is entered into by a corporate body that extends from Genesis to Revelation. Old world partners worshipped in the "beauty of holiness." Is this not still the mode? Along the line, others have witnessed to this truth.

Spurgeon wrote a wonderful treatise on Exodus 28:38 "the iniquity of the holy things." (He chronicled the "iniquities" of public worship in his own day: "hypocrisy, formality, luke warmness, irreverence, wandering of heart and forgetfulness of God.")[3] He declared all the work of the Lord done among them only amounted to: "selfishness, carelessness, slackness, unbelief, and a mass of defilement." Private devotions were characterized as: "a mass of dead earth" reeking in "laxity, coldness, neglect, sleepiness, and vanity." He pointed out that even the desire toward holiness was "polluted by ill motives." [4]

If this was the case in the early 1800's, what perfections have been made upon such atrocities in two-hundred years? Christian communities worldwide have developed a model of imperfection and semi-sanctification that literally rules in modern churchdom. Compromise-conditioned, its gospel is not the gospel of the Kingdom, for that kingdom is made up of saints, sanctified and functioning in holiness.

Albeit, the desire of the Almighty is not diminished by them or by time; He still demands holiness in the inward part. Just as the Old Testament Temple was designed for a holy people to come near a Holy God, the temple of the heart still must be housed in holiness. Worship can take place only in God defined holiness. Only when the holy constitute the chorus can there be any corporate worship which is acceptable to God. The holy know how to prepare for his Presence, please and praise Him.

Holy people greatly desire for their fleshly family to yield to the work of sanctification and join them. Paul, in Romans, willingly would have become "anathema" (sent to hell) in order for his people to know the Sanctifier of his own heart. All their religious trappings offered them substitute holiness when the Lord offered relational-holiness. Modern eyes weep for the same reason. When one realizes the portent of this revelation, it is no wonder he or she squirms in padded pews and twist in opera seats, longing for a breakthrough into all that God has provided in worship.

Paul sorrowfully acknowledged that his people were ignorant of what God had posited for them:

> ...Israelites, to whom pertain the adoption, the glory, the covenants, the giving of the law, the service of God and the promises;
> Romans 9:4 (NKJV)

Modern Christianity, likewise, is ignorant of all that God is willing to invest in them, not knowing that it is referenced and released through holiness.

Paul had renewed grief when he sighed under the realization:

> ....For they are not all Israel who are of Israel
> Romans 9:6 (NKJV)

Does this not grieve the Holy today? All are not Christian who are in the ranks of Christianity. Saints weep for what is missing. Much has been apportioned to those bearing the name "Believer" as well, for theirs is the Word, the gospel, the gifts of the Spirit and the many promises. Before the apportionment can be operative, believers must repent and embrace the sanctifying Spirit. Those who miss this, miss everything.

Paul could not fellowship with Israel, who had so many things in common with him, because they refused to be sanctified by His God. Today, the "holy" people languish for the same reason.

New Testament fellowship is based on Ephesians 2:19:

> Now, therefore, you are no longer strangers and foreigners, but <u>fellow citizens </u>with the <u>saints</u> and <u>members</u> of the household of God
> (NKJV)

139

Sadly, many who claim the label "Christian" are still strangers and foreigners.

Paul said earlier:

> He chose us in Him before the foundation of the world, <u>that</u> <u>we should be **holy** and with-</u><u>out blame</u> before Him in love, having predestinated us to adoption as sons by Jesus Christ Himself, according to the good pleasure of His will.   Ephesians 1:4-5 (NKJV)

Peter resounded similarly:

> As obedient children, not forming yourselves to the former lusts, as in your ignorance; but as He who called you is holy, <u>you also be holy</u> in all your conduct, because it is written, 'Be holy, for I am holy.'
>
>   I Peter 1:14-16 (NKJV)

Peter takes the case a step further when he exclaimed:

> …That through these you may be <u>partakers of</u> <u>the divine nature</u>….   II Peter 1:4 (NKJV)

A partaker is one who has the same feelings as the one he or she is partaker with, in this case, God. To have the "feelings of the divine" is a form of entering into "that which characterizes the Divine." A sharer, an associate are synonyms and are more intimate terms than is often denoted by "partaker." It is a Bride sort of thing. It is an identification that takes place like a bride who relishes being "Mrs. ____."

All the attributes of God's nature: love, truth, goodness, etc., are invested in the believer through the sanctifying power of God. Can it not be said of those who walk in holiness that they love with great love just as He does, that they hold to the truth tenaciously even as He, that they have goodness in their hearts and purity in their minds just like Him? Have they not

140

eclipsed the lusts of this world as they become the Branches and the Bride?

A holy relationship develops with the true believer's Lord when it expresses itself in his or her world, just like Jesus had relationship with the Father. "Partaker" means participating in His pleasure, that which excites Him, excites the saint. That which pleases Him, pleases them. The Branch is one with the vine; the Bride is married to the Bridegroom. It's a family thing, it's a connectivity thing; it's a deep down thing that makes one DIVINE! Partaking means having things in common with God, being a partner with Him.(Hebrews 12:23ff)

The *Song of Solomon* is a graphic picture of the development of sanctification in the life of the saint. The unfolding story of eight chapters ends with a perfect bride, ready to enter into Divine marriage. Between the first and the eighth chapter, one observes "bride development" which ranges from novice love at the beginning—to a mature sharing at the end. THIS IS the journey for the saint. Sanctification is not fiatly possessed; it is indeed an individual-relational process. No technical guide gives step by step method to attain it; it is relational; it has to be worked out.

In the "Song," the question is what transpired between the Shulamite and the King to cause her to cry out: "Let him possess the garden of my heart"? What formula, strictly followed, could there be which would lead to: " Set me as a seal upon your heart?" Two concise words appear to the heart as a possible answer. Repent and yield are the only two words which come to the mind of the sanctified. They have experienced the blessings that flow from such posture. John G. Lake, in writing about sanctification, expressed the essence of this transformation:

I believe the very beautiful thing we call SAL-VATION, and the holy statement of Jesus Christ, 'Ye must be born again," [John 3:7] is itself a scientific fact, and declaration of God's divine purpose and intent, based on the law of being. We are inclined to think that God just desires, and our hearts are changed. But I want to tell you, beloved, that there is a process in a man's soul that admits God into His life. Your heart opens because it is touched by the love of God, and into the heart, into the nature of man, there comes the divine essence of the living Spirit, and bless God, it has an action in him. Sin dissolves from his nature and from the mind of man. The Spirit of God takes possession of the cells of his brain, and his thoughts are changed by its action. There is a new realization of divine holiness. By the grace of God he discovers himself SANCTIFIED in deed and in truth, because Christ in truth dwells there.[5]

Lake's message is clear; the Holy Spirit transforms the mind and soul of man into a holy person. When the realization of this transmission surfaces in the heart of man, that man is at the threshold of the great promises and blessings waiting for him.

Holy Ones have been introduced to the treasures and blessings that follow commitment to their relationship. They have experienced a "holy kiss greeting" (I Thessalonians 5:26) among the "holy" brethren. They know what raising "holy hands" will do (I Timothy 2:8). Such hands have won enumerable battles, made the sun stand still, declared victory when defeat was man's conclusion, and lifted "most holy faith" prayers. Saints know what it means to stand on "holy" ground (Acts 7:33). They have already experienced His "holy" habitation: Exodus 15:13 (NKJV)

> You in Your mercy have led forth
> The people whom You have redeemed;
> You have guided them in Your strength
> <u>To Your holy habitation</u>.

Understanding Romans 11:16, they lay claim to their rootage and its life bearing flow.

> For if the first fruit is holy, the lump is also
> holy; and if the <u>root is holy</u>, so are the branches.

Spiritual genealogy yields no outlaws. Persons in this line are accustomed to hearing from God, whether by voice or vision. Present day saints also experience heavenly voice and "holy" vision, (Daniel 8:13ff, Psalms 89:19, Acts 16:9), for God speaks to them as He did to Daniel, David and Paul. The New Testament People were not peculiar in this; all who follow after them share in the Divine nature. What began with them, continues in all generations of the sanctified.

Saints know what comprises real prophesy and the difference between God's definition and man's fleshly version:

> for prophecy never came by the will of man,
> but <u>holy men </u>of God spoke as they were moved
> by the Holy Spirit.   II Peter 1:21(NKJV)

Saints know they are participating in a holy institution, reverenced by the holiness of God. Malachi 2:11 condemned Judah because they profaned it:

> ....For Judah has profaned the Lord's holy institution...

The Saint's holy institution is blessed by holy men and holy women (I Peter 3:5). They belong to a "holy" nation (I Peter 2:9) and live under a "holy" calling (II Tim 1:9). Instead of "church," they attend "holy" convocations (Leviticus 23:24). "Holy" conduct (II Peter 3:11) is blessed by "holy" law (Romans 7:12). Most "holy" faith energizes their prayers and the "holy" covenant keeps them (Luke 1:72). They have given their bodies as "holy" sacrifices realizing it is their reasonable service (Romans 12:1-2). A "holy" priesthood occupies their days and nights (I Peter 2:5, Leviticus 21:7-8), for they have a "holy" body ministry (Ephesians 5:27).

For Holy Ones, it is not enough to commune with "holy" angels (Rev. 14:10, Acts 10:22) and walk with "holy" men (II Peter 1:21). Do they not continue to climb the "holy" hill until they reach the "holy" city (Revelation 22:19,21:2)? Is not theirs the "holy" resurrection spoken of in Revelation 20:6? Is not theirs the "holy" apostles (Revelation 18:20), and have they not been shown God's "holy" arm (Isaiah 52:10)? Do they not hold a "holy" Bishopric (Titus 1:8) and preside under His "holy" Name (Ezekiel 43:7)? Such are they who honor, His Holiness!

.....'Holy, Holy, Holy,
Lord God Almighty,
Who was and is and is to come!'

Revelation 4:8

CHAPTER TEN

Righteous Determination

Do you not know that the unrighteous will not inherit
the kingdom of God?"
I Corinthians 6:9

Although this text does not find its way very often in religious literature, sermonic material or Bible study lessons, it is still scripture. Its message is simple and quiet clear. Its scope is far reaching in its import. Superceding all argumentation to the contrary, it allows for no vacillation, no wheedling or excuse for those who live in liberal moderation and/ or spiritual sedation. Succinctly stated in fourteen words, it means unless a person is righteous, that person will not be in heaven or be the recipient of kingdom promises.

Serendipity melts before its content, just as the religious message which abounds in cajoling psychology. Pulpits and counseling chambers have taken the tool of modern public education and declared everyone to be a "success" and a "champion." Somehow, the effort of many to hide behind such jargon (which attempts to assuage fear), finds little hope in the face of the realities looming across the horizon of mankind. Trying not to "upset" the congregation, the intent of modern pulpit panderers and religious professionals is to shield their constituency from any scripture which might be construed as "negative."

I Corinthians 6:9 is not a negative scripture, rather it is a positive propeller toward living a "righteous-determined" life. "Determined," as used in this case, means making every decision, every action, even every word—which proceeds from the mouth of the believer—righteous. The determining factor in any decision, any plan, word or deed will in effect be judged by, "Is it righteous?"

Those who accept the spiritual principle of "righteous-determinism" find laying before them vast promises, privileges, commanded blessings and an eternal kingdom. For those who do not, there is I Corinthians 6:9.

Recognizably, many people seek all kinds of avenues scripturally to avoid dealing with the Corinthian passage. These range from "there is none righteous, no not one (Romans 3:10—is a description of the unrighteous and unconverted)," to the theological premise: "all Old Testament uses of the word 'righteous' refer to external acts and not to the condition of the inward man." James decries the latter argument with, "Thus also faith by itself, if it does not have works, is dead (James 2:17)." Revelation patiently waits until the end to shatter the former with, "Let him who is righteous, be righteous still (indicative that the righteous will be alive and well on the earth in the last days [Revelation 22:11])." There **are** no excuses for not being righteous. Believers are not given a choice.

Pouring out of righteousness, the noun, is the adjective, righteous. As God or man moves into action, judgment positions itself in order to make a decree. Whether speech or hand, the first consideration of righteousness is whether or not the action or word is indeed righteous. A continual stream of judgment operates in the heart of the redeemed until righteousness reigns in the transformed heart. As transformation progresses, corrective judgment has to make fewer and fewer appearances and affirmative judgment presides. The Spirit dwelling within the righteous begins to hear testimony from without as He affirms the witness—"This One is righteous."

Glorious times are ahead for such as occupy this terrain. Earth becomes a showroom of light because the righteous always bring his or her deeds to the light. Riches accrue for the righteous soul, for hundreds of scriptures await to carry and bless him or her. (What of those who are not righteous? Fiery judgment accrues for them.)

Lingering in the shadows are literally millions who are unconvinced they can ever achieve this testimony. Misled by Twenty-first Century theology, they have either lost sight of even a distant possibility of such ranks being open to them or have been further convinced that no striving on their part is necessary (claiming all needed righteousness has been imputed to them). Both positions deprive the individual, whom Jesus purchased, from embracing a life of righteous-determination. In the former postulate, there is failure; in the latter, there is presumption (one of the great enemies of true righteousness).

Owning the character of a *Righteous-Being* carries the spirit of men and women to a foundation which makes them "steadfast and immoveable." Their works are not destined to flame; their heaven is not measured "so as by fire." This is why satan devises every plan possible to keep men and women from claiming this title. Satan seeks to keep mankind from exercising his or her righteousness (their inner resource) and producing that which is righteous (deeds, actions, words, Spirit controlled works). Satan knows two things can deter a righteous man: first, if he reaches for iniquity; and second, if he ceases to respond to the will of God. (Ezekiel was told to warn the righteous as well as the wicked.) The devil fears the righteous. Satan knows righteous people are as "bold as a lion (Proverbs 28:1)." The toothless, roaring lion doesn't want to face a righteous one! When a soul becomes "righteous-determined," he or she moves into a realm of spiritual claim that offers assurance from and fellowship with the Lord—a place where satan cannot travel. Positioned in power, huge rivers of life flow through the spirits of righteous men and women. Their desire is that of Amos.

> Let justice run down like water,
> And righteousness like a mighty stream.
>
> Amos 5:24 (NKJV)

The real movers and shakers on this earth are "the righteous," for they are the ones trusted by the Lord. Righteous acts must be done on earth by righteous souls in order to glorify their Righteous God. In such a context, righteous men and women must not only exist, they must be active in the earth. The evil one has overwhelmed religious theology by teaching: "When one gets to heaven, he or she will be perfected and attain the 'righteous' state." That is Hinduism not Christianity! (Righteous people are duty bound to stand against such teaching, to bring about a great awakening to the true purpose of God—to bring upon the earth a people like Himself.)

Some of the greatest corrective forces in history have been "awakening" to the principles of righteousness. Such a spiritual "awakening" preceded the birth of the United States.

Theodorus Jacobus Frelinghuysen (1691-1748), a Dutch reform preacher ministering in New Jersey, began preaching on personal-experience-righteousness. His message was an affront to the lethargy of his day. He preached what historians termed "Pietism." Soon the religious world was divided between "New Lights" and "Old Lights."[1] The "New Lights" shone so bright that the "Old Lights" seemed like darkness. Institutions changed, a solidifying of communities began to follow, and the winds of nationalism birthed a nation of free men. (Perhaps it should be the obligation of every person who is a citizen of the United States [natural born or from foreign soil] to visit Jamestown's Cross and Church and study the "Great Awakening" of the 1700's.)

Frehlinghusen yielded to the Spirit of God and began to preach from passages like I Peter 4:18. (His messages revealed the necessity to preach contrarian scriptures to the standard texts used by established churches.) The religious norm was deemed "not normal" to him, as he projected that being an "Average Christian" was a ticket to damnation.

In deference to the recent cleric who exclaimed, "I am tired of hearing messages using ministers of a hundred years ago as authority. What I have to say is current; what they had to say is outdated. I don't have time to familiarize myself with their teaching either, because I have more recent revelation of my own," Frelinghuysen ministered more than two hundred years ago.

Hear this progenitor of the "New Light" lay the biblical foundations for being righteous, using for a text a scripture virtually unheard in modern times: I Peter 4:18 "and if the righteous are scarcely saved, where shall the ungodly and the sinner appear?" He began by arguing that the salvation provided by Jesus Christ wrought more than what was demonstrated by the "church attendees" of his day. Christ's salvation included a work leading to a holy and righteous person.

> 'Is it true, my hearers, that the righteous are scarcely and with so much difficulty saved? It

149

becomes us then not to esteem salvation so lightly and of such easy attainment. Unless we would directly oppose the Word of God, we must acknowledge salvation to be a quite different thing from what is supposed by most men who yet hope to be saved; for they imagine that it is entirely well with them, and that they shall be saved provided they avoid outward and gross sins, live honest and correct lives, perform the external duties of godliness, and diligently pursue the business of their calling. 0 wretched men! Can that be true godliness and the narrow way of life? No! Oh, No! Outwardly to forsake sin, pursue virtue, and live correctly is only in accordance with the practice of the heathen, as said the Saviour, 'Do not even the Publicans so?

(Matthew 5:47).'[2]

Ah, Ha,! the circle has been completed; for just as Frehinhuysen's generation turned to the "New Light," the early days of the Twenty first-Century find this generation returning to "Old Light" darkness. Few seek to be righteous, and the curriculum of the church is fortified by the Antiseptic Skeptics who not only live contrary to the Word, but promote the same. Their tasteless diatribe is heard on television and from the pulpit, all of it bearing such similarity that it smacks of conspiracy. Their message has become the "standard for and of the religious community."

T.A. Frelinghuysen was not satisfied with "standard religion:"

'They do not carefully examine **whether they are righteous** and are not concerned whether they are in a state of grace and have an inter-

150

est in Christ, but satisfy themselves with a bare and unfounded persuasion and place dependence upon the external propriety of their conduct. They rely upon the fact that they are baptized, that they have made confession of their faith, that they partake of the Lord's supper, that they attend the house of God and read His Word, Upon these things, I say, they rely and, in the meanwhile, are groveling as very motes, and this but to acquire some earthly goal and entertain not the slightest doubt that they shall be saved. This they regard as certain! But know, 0 vain man, that thou shall not thus attain salvation! These things must indeed be done but are not in themselves sufficient. The Spirit of God declares by the mouth of Peter that the **righteous** are but scarcely saved. Do you expect so easily to secure it? Oh, no! You lamentably deceive yourself and greatly err.'[3]

Frelinghuysen was saying what must be said today, "Redeemed man must '**be**' righteous through faith in Jesus." Yes, he believed in "imputed" righteousness (right standing with God which comes in salvation), but went on to emphasize that it manifested itself in the believer **actually being** "righteous."

The **righteous** are such as also conduct themselves agreeably to this **righteousness** and do what is right and proper according to the law of God and thus are 'filled with the **fruits of Righteousness**' (Philippians 1:11). They are such as are hereupon also justified in their own consciences through their good works and that holy frame of mind of which they are con-

151

scious, as a fruit of their uprightness and faith; with whose spirit the Spirit of God beareth witness, that they are the children of God (Romans *8:16*). *They also show, by their holy lives, that they <u>are</u> righteous* and thus are **justified in the consciences of others and recognized as such.** These are the children of God—believers and such as are in covenant with God."[4]

Is it strange that he alludes to the witness-triangle to verify a person as "righteous?" The world, the church and God acknowledge and testify through inward and outward evidence of the "righteous" reality. Righteous men and women do exist on this earth, and those who swell their ranks are those who have the testimony of God within their spirit and who have similar testimony from others.

T.A.Frehlinghusen explored the ramifications of I Peter 4:18, tendering to his audience that "scarcely" means "with much difficulty," both on man and God's part. A brief recapping of his major theses is sufficient to show his direction:

1. The righteous are those who are "in" faith "with" Jesus Christ.

2. The righteous are those who are sanctified by the Spirit of God, "who do righteousness" (I John 3:7), "follow after righteousness" (I Timothy 6:11), and "walk in all the ordinances and commandments of the Lord" (Luke 1:6).

3. It is certain that the righteous are saved, and they only.

4. (paraphrasing) Great difficulty comes when man realizes he is a sinner and he can bring nothing to the equation. If he be saved, he must exercise repentance in accordance with Luke 13:3 (He must actually repent). And what does this act of the soul include? It

includes a turning from **sin to holiness**, from Satan to God, from ourselves and all creatures **unto Christ.** Given the massive affront of ungodliness in the world, this is with great difficulty.

5.   ... a work of great difficulty occurs to cause a sinner to entertain that confidence in God without which he cannot be led to repentance; thus, he Is scarcely saved. **If he shall be saved, he must be made holy**; for without holiness no man shall see the Lord (Hebrews 12:14). And what a work this is!

What energy and skill must the Holy Ghost employ to sanctify the elect sinner. (This smacked the "easy believe-ism of his day in the mouth.)

6.   Thus he must not only be sanctified in all that he does and leaves undone, yield his members as <u>instruments of righteousness</u>, and to this end forsake all things (cutting off a right hand and plucking out a right eye (Matthew 6), that is, abandoning his dearest bosom sins), but he must be **inwardly sanctified**, his heart must be changed (entirely transformed), and the image of God impressed upon it. He must be holy in all his motives in order to glorify God in all things. And oh! How great the work to sanctify a heart so habituated to sin, vanity, and folly and to impart to it true wisdom. To effect this, naught less than divine power is adequate...

7.   Inasmuch as he must be heavenly minded and willing to part with all that is seen for that which is unseen, if he be saved it must be with difficulty. With Paul he *must count* all things but dung for the excellency of the knowledge of Christ (Philippians 3:8). He must despise the favor of men, the treasures, riches, and delights of the world, and seek only those

153

things which are above, where Christ is, thus exalting the Lord Jesus above ten thousand and so proclaim Him to the world. But oh, the magnitude of such a work!

8.   God sometimes tests the righteous. He seemingly-abandons them to bring them to a greater understanding of Himself. The righteous are the only ones who care about the closeness of God or yearn for His presence, herein is the difference garnered between those who are and are not! (summary)

9.   The world is diametrically opposed to the righteous: Hence their wrestling, their watching, their praying against sin, their tears, sorrows, and complaints, with Paul, 'O wretched man that I am! Who shall deliver me from the body of this death?' (Romans 7:24). ...for many are the the kingdom of God (Acts 14:22). Thus also must a child of God, in the work of salvation, strive against enemies so numerous and with violence assault the kingdom of heaven (Matthew 11-2); run in the Christian race (I Corinthians 9:24); **follow after perfection** (Philippians 3:12); and exercise him self unto godliness (I Timothy 4:7). This last, literally expressed**, is wrestling**."[5]

Is it any wonder the middle colonies experienced an "awakening" termed "Great"? One by one, the hearers took to heart this message of personal-righteous-living. Living the righteous life became something embraceable, something real to them. Opposed to liturgical stoicism, theirs was a restoration of the purpose and plan of God for his redeemed man. (God wants a people like Himself upon the earth.)

A Great Awakening needs to occur in the Twenty-first Century! Something far afield from current seminars, bonding camps and women's meetings must occur. Deeper than what has passed for Godliness, defined by modern standards, it must include a state of being which delivers the soul of man to the continual presence of the Mighty One. It must offer a fellowship in the redeemed which is not experienced in church socials and contrived gatherings; it must lay hold to what Zacharias and Elizabeth knew:

> There was in the days of Herod, the king of Judea, a certain priest named Zacharias, of the division of Abijah. His wife was of the daughters of Aaron, and her name was Elizabeth. **And they were** both righteous before God, walking in all the commandments **and ordinances of the Lord blameless.** But they had no child, because Elizabeth was barren, and they were both well advanced in years.
>
> Luke 1:5-7 (NKJV)

Their son, John the Baptist, grew up in a family of righteous parents. Is it any wonder a "great awakening" swept the countryside when he began his ministry? Religious leaders were his converts, and they, along with the masses, humbly were immersed. Families today need the testimony of parents, "They (are) were both righteous before God," but few have it. When this occurs, miracles will happen for them, and their children will bring many to repentance.

It is time to lay hold on these scriptures:

> And now, little children, abide in Him, that when He appears, we may have confidence and not be ashamed before Him at His coming. If you know **that He is righteous**, you know that everyone who **practices righteousness** is born of Him.   1 John 2:28-29 (NKJV)

Little children, let no one deceive you. **He who practices righteousness is righteous**, just as He is righteous.   1 John 3:7 (NKJV)

Righteous-determinism's litmus is pragmatic, not liturgical!

CHAPTER ELEVEN

Determined To Be Righteous

For the ways of the LORD are right;
The righteous walk in them. Hosea 14:9
The name of the LORD is a strong tower;
The righteous run to it and are safe. Prov.18:10

Righteous-determinism begins with a resolve of the spirit;
there must be an inner determination to be a righteous
person. With this, the meanderings of the ordinary will be a
thing of the past. Instilled in the righteous spirit is a knowledge showing how God intends to have a people like Him.
His word is explicit as to what will be their character, the
commands that they must follow, the privileges they will enjoy and the promises they must hold to.

It is the righteous who prophesy in truth, the righteous
who pray and the universe is changed, the righteous who commune with one another on a level in the Spirit which
supercedes the communication of unredeemed beings—to the
righteous belongs the kingdom.

Scripture is not slack in determining the characteristics

of the righteous. Beginning in Genesis, foundations were laid for this holy people.

> By faith Abel offered to God a more excellent sacrifice than Cain, through which he obtained witness that <u>he was righteous</u>, God testifying of his gifts; and through it he being dead still speaks.   Hebrews 11:4 (NKJV) (Genesis 4)
>
> Not as Cain who was of the wicked one and murdered his brother. And why did he murder him? Because his works were evil and his brother's <u>righteous</u>.   1 John 3:12 (NKJV)

Likewise an Old Testament event is reviewed in II Peter:

> and delivered **righteous Lot**, who was oppressed by the filthy conduct of the wicked (for that **righteous** man, dwelling among them, tormented **his righteous soul** from day to day by seeing and hearing their lawless deeds)— then the Lord knows how to deliver the **godly** out of temptations….
>   2 Peter 2:6-9 (NKJV) (Genesis 18-19)

To those who claim all righteousness in the Old Testament is tied only to righteous acts, or deeds, these two passages juxtapose one another. ("Godly," is Bible-defined as "righteous.")

These men possessed the <u>state of being</u> known as "righteous." Are there no more like them or have they all perished from the earth? Are there none to which society and religion can look today and find example? Doubtless, Peter and the author of Hebrews did not think so!

Simon, in his work, defined the righteous—by specifically defining the "unrighteous." Unrighteous behavior was seen as a condition which issued from a heart of unrighteousness. Therefore, the same was true for the righ-

158

teous—that which is righteous (adjective) comes from a heart of righteousness (noun).

Paul defined "righteous" acts as the result of a heart of righteousness. Jesus established a similar foundation for the righteous in Paul's letter to the Ephesians (2:19). He answered the cogent question raised a thousand years before:

> If the foundations are destroyed,
> What can the righteous do?
>
> Psalms 11:3 (NKJV)

The foundations have been destroyed, and those who lead and attend churches are largely responsible. How? By refusing to teach the high standards of God and by excepting that which is unacceptable to Him. They have sculpted a false sense of what is righteous. They have substituted their form of the righteous for God's true form. Substitution has denied the believer opportunity to enter the realm of the truly righteous and to enjoy a heritage in the saints which far exceeds modern terms.

The insidious smile of a church greeter is no substitute for the rejoicing of the righteous!

> The voice of rejoicing and salvation
> Is in the tents of the righteous;
>
> Psalms 118:15 (NKJV)

Seeking to rectify some of the substitution of modern religion, Colin Melbourne, English Missionary in Asia, wrote about perfecting righteousness in the life of the believer:

> There is a place in Christ Jesus where we no longer live under condemnation, but where Heaven is always open to us. A place of limit-less power, untold resources, and Divine LIFE. Everything we need, to give us total victory over all the power of the Devil. Nothing can

159

stop the child of God, filled with desire to press
on into this life of true holiness, desiring only
to glorify God.[1]

Melbourne correctly interprets John 17 and Jesus' Priestly
Prayer as being an intercession for His followers in order for
them to be one, individually, with the Father just as He is one
with Father. When this is consummated, Christ's righteousness becomes something one owns, like other spiritual pos-
sessions.

I pray this also for those who will believe in
me... that all of them may be one, Father, just
as you are in me, and I am in you. May they
also be in us ....**that they may be one as we
are one. I in them, and you in me.**
John. 17:20-23 (NKJV)

Vistas will open for the child of God who grasps this truth!
God's promises to him or her can be possessed; they can claim
spiritual ownership. Such ownership is a non-entity to the
majority of the religious world. Multitudes who attend ser-
vices, fill seminars and occupy church positions have no con-
ception about owning scripture and possessing promises, let
alone embodying righteousness. For instance, what happens
when one grasps the promise of the following Psalm and
moves on its promise?

The <u>righteous</u> cry out, and the LORD hears,
And delivers them out of all their troubles.
The LORD is <u>near</u> to those who **have a
broken heart,**
And saves such **as have a contrite spirit.**
Psalms 34:17-18 (NKJV)

Owning such treasure-scripture is the portion of the righteous (those who have a broken heart and contrite spirit), and

satan has sought to rob and steal what rightfully belongs to them. Here are other Scriptures displaying righteous attributes that can be equally possessed. As one reads each verse, an awareness will arise alongside the truth of the verse—an awareness that these verses can belong to him or her. They can claim them, pray them back to the Father, include them in their conversation, teach them to children and grandchildren.

Proverbs 15:6 In the house of the righteous there **is** much treasure

Proverbs 10:11 The mouth of the righteous **is** a well of life

Proverbs 10:16 The labor of the righteous leads to life

Proverbs 10:20 The tongue of the righteous **is** choice silver

Proverbs 10:21 The lips of the righteous **feed** many

Proverbs 10:32 The lips of the righteous **know** what is acceptable

Proverbs 11:9b-10 through knowledge the righteous **will be** delivered. When it goes well with the righteous, the city rejoices

Proverbs 11:23 The desire of the righteous is only good

Proverbs 11:30 The fruit of the righteous **is** a tree of life

Proverbs 12:3 the root of the righteous **cannot** be moved

Proverbs 12:5 The thoughts of the righteous **are** right

Proverbs 12:12 the root of the righteous **yields** fruit

161

Proverbs 13:25 the righteous **eats** to the satisfying of his soul

Proverbs 15:28 The heart of the righteous **studies** how to answer

Proverbs 20:7 the righteous man **walks** in his integrity; His children **are** blessed after him.

Proverbs 21:26 But **the righteous gives** and does not spare

Proverbs 24:16 For a <u>righteous man (or woman)</u>may fall seven imes And **rise again**

Proverbs 29:6-7 By transgression an evil man is snared,

But the **righteous sings and rejoices**. The righteous **considers** the cause of the poor

Psalms 37:21 b the righteous **shows mercy** and gives

Psalms 37:30 The mouth of the righteous **speaks wisdom**

The righteous person can claim these attributes as his or her own, but it is error to wholesalely cover audiences with these venues! True believers can walk in these verses, but not without righteous determination. (Highlighted in bold are key words, many times signifying a transaction has already taken place or an attribute which is operative presently in the heart of the righteous.) "Surely there <u>is</u> **a reward** for the righteous; Surely He is God who judges in the earth (Psalms 58:11)."

The righteous **will be** in everlasting remembrance.

He **will not** be afraid of evil tidings;

His heart **is** steadfast, trusting in the LORD.

His heart **is** established; He will not be afraid,

Until **he sees** his desire upon his enemies.

Psalms 112:6b-8 (NKJV)

162

Salient need cries out to this generation, "Let there again be discernment between those who are righteous and those who are not." Tares have been sown among the wheat, but the harvest time quickly approaches when separation will be necessary.

> Then you shall again discern
> Between the righteous and the wicked,
> Between one who serves God
> And one who does not serve Him
>
> Mal 3:18 (NKJV)

Jesus said it another way: He said the judgment at the end of time will provide opportunity to let the righteous shine forth. His kingdom currently has tares, but not for long.

> The enemy who sowed them is the devil, the harvest is the end of the age, and the reapers are the angels. Therefore as the tares are gathered and burned in the fire, so it will be at the end of this age. The Son of Man will send out His angels, and they will gather **out of His kingdom** all things that offend, and those who practice lawlessness, and will cast them into the furnace of fire. There will be wailing and gnashing of teeth. ***Then the righteous*** **will shine** forth as the sun in the kingdom of their Father. He who has ears to hear, let him hear!
>
> Matthew 13:39-43 (NKJV)

Muted by tares for a little while longer, the hour will soon arrive when the righteous will shine forth as the sun. These are they who receive the promises and make them their own. (The Holy Spirit will make these promises sure to their heart, therefore they should be read purposefully and not in haste.)

163

1 Peter 3:12 For the <u>eyes</u> of the LORD are <u>on</u> <u>the righteous,</u>

And His <u>ears</u> are <u>open to their prayers;</u>

James 5:16-18 The effective, fervent prayer of a righteous man avails much. Elijah was a man with a nature like ours, and he prayed earnestly that it would not rain; and it did not rain on the land for three years and six months. And he prayed again, and the heaven gave rain, and the earth produced its fruit.

Psalms 5:12 You, O LORD, will <u>bless the righteous</u>

Psalms 14:5 God is **with** the generation of the righteous.

Psalms 34:15 The eyes of the LORD are on the righteous

Psalms37:17 But the LORD **upholds** the righteous

Psalms 37:39-40 But the salvation of the righteous is from the LORD; He is their strength in the time of trouble. And the LORD shall help them and deliver them; He shall deliver them from the wicked, And save them, Because they trust in Him

Psalms 55:22b He shall never permit the righteous to be moved

Psalms 92:12-14 The righteous shall flourish like a palm tree, He shall grow like a cedar in Lebanon. Those who are planted in the house of the LORD Shall flourish in the courts of our God. They shall still bear fruit in old age They shall be fresh and flourishing

Psalms 146:8 The LORD loves the righteous

Proverbs 10:3 The LORD will not allow the righteous soul to famish

Proverbs 10:24 And the desire of the righteous will be granted

Proverbs 10:25 But the righteous has an everlasting foundation.

Proverbs 10:28 The hope of the righteous will be gladness

Proverbs 10:30 The righteous will never be removed

Proverbs 11:8-10 The righteous **is** delivered from trouble, And it comes to the wicked instead

Proverbs 11:21 the posterity of the righteous **will be** delivered.

Proverbs 11:28 the righteous **will** flourish like foliage

Proverbs 12:7 the house of the righteous **will** stand

Proverbs 12:13 the righteous **will** come through trouble

Proverbs 12:21 no grave trouble **will** overtake the righteous

Proverbs 13:21-22 to the righteous, good **shall be** repaid

A good man leaves an inheritance to his children's children, But the wealth of the sinner is stored up for the righteous.

Proverbs 14:32 the righteous **has** a refuge in his death

Proverbs 15:29 The LORD is far from the wicked,

But He hears the prayer of the righteous.

165

> Psalms 37:25-26 I have been young, and now
> am old;
> Yet I have not seen the righteous forsaken,
> Nor his descendants begging bread.
> He is ever merciful, and lends;
> And his descendants are blessed
> Proverbs 18:10 The name of the LORD is a
> strong tower;
> The righteous run to it and are safe.
> Psalms 97:11-12 Light is sown for the righ-
> teous, And gladness for the upright in heart

Prolific promises and rewards are the lot of the righteous and nearly all of them are for earth life. God knows those who are His (He has earth intimacy with His righteous ones). With God there is no middle ground, no such thing as being half-righteous and half unrighteous. One is either righteous or not. To the righteous belong these verses, to those who are not—they do not belong.

Foolishly, ministries have patented concepts and built assurances upon these scriptures (which are clearly ONLY for the righteous) which they have promised to everyone. This is sin. The righteous know in their inner heart who they are, but the majority of the religious do not possess this witness. Their marginal spiritual life has left them in anomie. They fail the testing of the Lord.

The righteous are they who can pass God's tests.

> Jeremiah 20:12 (NKJV) But, O LORD of
> hosts,
> You who **test** the righteous, And see the
> mind and heart
> Psalms 1:6 For the LORD knows the way of
> the righteous
> Psalms 7:9 For the righteous God **tests** the
> hearts and minds

Psalms 11:5 the LORD **tests** the righteous, But the wicked and the one who loves violence His soul hates.

1 Thessalonians 2:4-5 But as we have been approved by God to be entrusted with the gospel, even so we speak, not as pleasing men, but God who **tests** our hearts.

Matt 25:37-41 Then the **righteous will answer** Him, saying, Lord, when did we see You hungry and feed You, or thirsty and give You drink? When did we see You a stranger and take You in, or naked and clothe You? Or when did we see You sick, or in prison, and come to You? And the King will answer and say to them, Assuredly, I say to you, inasmuch as you did it to one of the least of these My brethren, you did it to Me.

The righteous can answer, for the righteous are these who have responded to Him, know His voice and love Him. Spiritual answers are within them. The Spirit has been their School Master and their recitations are perfect.

These distinctions must be forcibly brought to the at-large church. Righteousness must be preached in every pulpit, taught in every classroom, power-pointed on the walls of cathedrals and halls—until the congregation, the classes and the recipients are righteous! The Spirit would have it so!

Concomitant to these "righteous ones" are certain commandments which they alone can accomplish. It takes **being** righteous to carry out command-scriptures directed to them.

Be glad in the LORD and rejoice, **you righteous**;

And shout for joy, all you upright in heart!

Psalms 32:11 (NKJV)

167

The rejoicing of the righteous, the shouting of the righteous is not only commanded, it is distinctive. Not everyone can fulfill this kind of rejoicing and shouting. Many feign it— Sunday by Sunday, but only the righteous can do it right! Rejoicing done by them has a degree of power which cannot be attained by those who are not. Righteous rejoicing is different! Attendant blessings follow their obedience, for the Lord does specific things for the benefit of the righteous.

> Light is sown for the righteous,
> And gladness for the upright in heart.
> Rejoice in the LORD, you righteous,
> And give thanks at the remembrance of His
> holy name.
>
> Psalms 97:11-12 (NKJV)

In the two former examples, rejoicing became a "righteous requirement" for those concerned with the command of the Lord. Paul speaks of the righteous requirement of the Law and how Jesus fulfilled those requirements. Those who follow Christ find themselves faced with their own righteous requirements from the Lord which exceed those established by organized religion. (Such was precisely addressed when Jesus gave the parable of the good Samaritan. Religion passed up what the righteous Samaritan could not.)

The righteous live with greater concerns, deeper levels of commitment and sensitivity to the will and purpose of God than "people of religion." Their prayers are pro-active, their work redemptive, their yearnings creative (calling those things into being which are not), their prospective broader (often worldwide), their vision clearer (light is sown for them), their path productive (the Lord directs) and their progress assured.

> …that the **righteous requirement** of the law
> might be fulfilled in us who do not walk according to the flesh but according to the Spirit.
>
> Romans 8:4 (NKJV)

Righteous people fast and pray while others relax and recreate. They walk in spiritual angst, seeking answers from God, while others see no need (David's prayer for guidance I Samuel 23:9-12 is counterpoised to Saul's insidious blessing toward an informant, "Blessed are you of the Lord, for you have had compassion on me [while harboring the religious intent of killing David] I Samuel 23:21)." David soon learned the trials brought on by being righteous. The scripture details his adventures with the purpose of illustrating the great opposition that arises when men and women determine to follow God in righteousness.

The agencies of man and the church cannot abide the truly righteous.

Many are the afflictions of the righteous,
But the LORD delivers him out of them all.
                    Psalms 34:19 (NKJV)

The wicked watches the righteous,
And seeks to slay him.
                    Psalms 37:32(NKJV)

All the horns (power) of the wicked I will also
    cut off,
But the horns of the righteous shall be exalted.
                    Psalms 75:10(NKJV)

Shall the throne of iniquity, which devises evil
    by law,
Have fellowship with You?
They gather together against the life of the righteous,
And condemn innocent blood.
But the LORD has been my defense,
And my God the rock of my refuge.
                    Psalms 94:20-22 (NKJV)

The most misunderstood group in the annals of history are the righteous. Their hearts are knit with the heart of God, for they have the same accolade as David, "a man (or woman) after God's own heart." To be righteous is a heart thing! Most of the "religious" cannot comprehend this. Their crass criticisms rail against the righteous but will be severely dealt with:

> Let the lying lips be put to silence,
> Which speak insolent things **proudly and contemptuously against the righteous**.
>
> Psalms 31:18

(All the heart rendering of Psalms 69 precedes the following verses; they pray curses on those who fight against the Lord's people.)

> Add iniquity to their iniquity,
> Let them not come into Your righteousness,
> Let them be blotted out of the book of the living,
> And not be <u>written with the righteous</u>
>
> Psalms 69:27b-28 (NKJV)

Crying from a righteous spirit, David declared:

> Because zeal for Your house has eaten me up,
> And the reproaches of those who reproach You
>   has fallen on me.   Psalms 69:9(NKJV)

Is this not the soul sound of every righteous being on the face of the earth? While viewing the moral and ethical travesties of society, their faces turn to religious ravishing, and with brokenness and tears they fall to their knees and exclaim, "The reproaches of those who reproach You has fallen on me."

Because their spiritual walk has so often thrust the truly righteous into contact with numerous religious institutions,

Righteous souls soon determine to be divested of all religious trappings. They refuse to associate with or to embrace the profane, whether in walk or in object. (Sometimes it has been necessary to cast from their workplace and homes, images or art objects. These may seem be harmless items, but ones the Holy Spirit has identified "with other spirits.") Many more have had to close ranks and exclude business, social and church friendships. Sadly, the righteous must review the state of the house of God in the same way David did, "The zeal **for** Your house has eaten me up." They cannot glibly pass by, for their souls cry out when they encounter the pathetic state of the church. The righteous care! They are different!

Almost every aspect of the earth-walk is different for the righteous. Their understanding of the Word, their focus in life, their hopes and dreams, their view of history (as well as current events), their conversation, their view of reality, their relationship to Jesus, the Father and the Holy Spirit, the way they relate to others, their scope of wisdom and spiritual understanding, the depth of their bearing in public and private and their overall sensitivity to the things of God are different than "religion man." They are different!

The righteous are a people the world cannot do without, for Spirit-work can only be accomplished by them. When they enter a situation, the situation changes; theirs is a power divested of self. All reward is based on their work; all their work originates with Him.

> He who receives you receives Me, and he who receives Me receives Him who sent Me. He who receives a prophet in the name of a prophet shall receive a prophet's reward. And he who receives a <u>righteous man </u>in the name of a righteous man (Jesus, the righteous) shall <u>receive a righteous man's reward</u>.
>
> Matthew 10:40-41 (NKJV)

CHAPTER TWELVE

H & R Power

Those who do wickedly against the covenant
he shall corrupt with flattery; but the <u>people who know
their God shall be strong, and carry out great exploits</u>.
And those of the people
who understand shall instruct many; yet for
many days they shall fall by sword and
flame, by captivity and plundering.
Now when they fall, they shall be aided
with a little help; but many shall join
with them by intrigue. And some of those of
understanding shall fall, to refine them,
purify them, and make them white,
until the time of the end; because it is still
for the appointed time.
Daniel 11:31-35 (NKJV)

The Lord did not redeem His people in order for them
to be ordinary. Nothing in Scripture allows the follower
of God to be average, mundane, restive or drawn back.

Throughout the Bible, those persons who pleased God were people of faith, but they possessed a faith that did not stop short of the glory of God. They knew something that the "faith folks" of this century have either forgotten or possibly never knew. They knew the end results of faith were deeds called up by righteousness and spawned by holiness. Since all things reported or acknowledged in the Word are for the glory of God, then Daniel's "saint-exploits" must also be for God's glory. Exploits are the craft of holy and righteous people. Exploits are the expected work of the saints. They have "exploit-faith," the kind of faith that draws the believer INTO the person of Jesus Christ and God, the Father. The Almighty is known for His exploits, so must His people be thusly known.

This God-kind of holiness and righteousness-faith becomes the faith which operates in all those truly redeemed. No, the created does not become the creator, what they become, by entering into His faith realm, is a creature who can say like Paul, "Imitate me, just as I also imitate Christ (I Corinthians 11:1)." In other words, "The righteousness that is in Him is in me." "The holiness in Him is in me." "Just as the scripture found fulfillment in Jesus, the scripture finds fulfillment in me." "Just as He was focused on a place beyond this earth, so I am focused on a place beyond earth." "Find a quality in Him and you will see it working in me!" "If He prayed in a garden, I will dare pray in one." "If He was willing to die to fulfill the will of God for His life, I too am willing to follow the will of God unto death." "If He promised perfection of righteousness and holiness, I am a recipient of that promise."

Paul in essence was saying, "If you are looking for someone in whom the Holy Spirit is spawning exploits, look at me." Are there those with a similar testimony today?

Seemingly no one is willing to take the step of faith Paul

took—at least not in the Twenty-first Century. Nay, the super awareness of falling religious stars has swept clean the stage of the supernatural. Yet, others in Biblical history took that step. David dared many times to write he was both righteous and holy (if one examines the Psalms). Ten thousand dead were scattered on his battle fields; many wives and concubines (including Bathsheba) were in his harem; the death of an illegitimate child stood before him in Nathanic judgment, yet he was "a man after God's own heart." Someone might question his validity, "How dare he speak!" Nevertheless, here are his words:

> Open to me the gates of Righteousness,
> I will go through them,
> And I will praise the Lord,
> Through which the righteous shall enter
> > Psalms 118:19 (NKJV)
> Preserve my life, for I am holy
> > Psalms 86:2 (NKJV)

Where are those like David today? Where are those who will verbalize their soul and declare who they are? Is there something amiss in a religious society which continually recites the promises of faith-Scripture while never declaring one is perfected by it? For instance, why are there so many who are quick to teach on tongues and prophesy and cite every Pauline verse they can possibly squeeze into their books, seminars and sessions, yet never say a word about I Corinthians 14:25?

Paul said the unbeliever will "have the secrets of his heart revealed, and so, falling down on his face; will worship God and REPORT that GOD IS TRULY AMONG YOU." Could it be that such activities do not have these results in the Twenty-first Century? Could it be that Christendom has so distanced itself from the purposes of God that excuses suffice for the absence of such activity, or does this scripture no longer ap-

ply? Tongues, prophesy and falling sinners are connected together, just as Hebrews eleven is connected to Hebrews twelve.

Hebrews eleven was written before Hebrews twelve for a
reason! Men and women who possessed the kind of faith spoken of in chapter eleven are shown perfected in chapter twelve.
Their exploits are revealed in Hebrews eleven, but the end of
their faith-exploits is found in chapter twelve. Faith defined
in chapter eleven holds in its hands its finished work in chapter twelve: righteousness and holiness.

Every act of faith portrayed in the great "hall of faith (He-
brews11)," led that person to possess the "fruit of righteousness (Hebrews 12:11)" and own "holiness (Hebrews 12:14)."
The "great cloud of witnesses" of Hebrews 12:1 challenges
the faintest of souls to rise up and cast off every weight and
ensnaring sin in order to muster with them.

If the righteous and holy are to judge the nations, govern
the earth and reign with the King of Righteousness, how then
can they fail to be examples alongside those of history who
are the "great cloud?" If one scrutinizes each hero of faith
cited in chapter eleven, he or she will find elements of chapter twelve, holiness and righteousness, in them.

Abel, of faith, "obtained witness that he was RIGHTEOUS
(Hebrews 11:4)." Enoch, in faith, was translated into the presence of God, a matter impossible without holiness according
to Hebrews 12:14. Jude even listed Enoch as one who prophesied about the coming of the end-time "holiness" folk.

Noah, "became heir of the righteousness which is according to faith (Hebrews 11:7)." (Faith-righteousness is a silent
theme in current circles.) Simon Peter called Naoh "a preacher
of righteousness (II Peter 2:5)," a breed almost extinct in
modern times. Gen 6:9 said, "Noah was a just man, perfect in
his generations." Few strive for perfection in these last days,
which are like the days of Noah. The scriptures summarize

his biography in four words, "Noah walked with God." Ezekiel 14:14 unequivocally crowned three men as possessing righteousness, "Even if these three men, Noah, Daniel, and Job, were in it, they would deliver only themselves by *their* righteousness, says the Lord GOD." (Someone must exhibit *his or her* righteousness today, lest this generation perish for lack of an example.)

Abraham, spoken of 232 times in Scripture, had this report in James 2:22-24:

> And the Scripture was fulfilled which says, Abraham believed God, and it was accounted to him for righteousness. And he was called the friend of God. You see then that a man is justified by works, and not by faith only.
>
> (NKJV)

> Therefore He who supplies the Spirit to you and works **miracles among you,** does He do it by the works of the law, or by the hearing of faith?— just as Abraham "believed God, and it was accounted to him for righteousness." Therefore know that only those who are of faith are sons of Abraham. And the Scripture, foreseeing that God would justify the Gentiles by faith, preached the gospel to Abraham beforehand, saying, 'In you all the nations shall be blessed.' So then those who are of faith are blessed with believing Abraham.
>
> Gal 3:5-9 (NKJV)

(An aside for this verse, might be a question: "Where are the 'miracles among you' today?" Perhaps so great an emphasis has been placed on "imputed righteousness," and so little emphasis on the "miracles among you," the religious world has lost their connection.)

177

Isaac, one of "the great cloud of witnesses," was promised the blessing of Abraham:

> And give you the blessing of Abraham
>
> Gen 28:4 (NKJV)

> 'In Isaac your seed shall be called.' That is, those who are the children of the flesh, these are not the children of God; but the <u>children of the promise</u> are counted as the seed.
>
> Romans 9:7 (NKJV)

The confession of the redeemed should be, " I am a seed of the promise." The vast lineage of the "heritage anointing" comes to the children of God, not the children of flesh.

Jacob joined that special line and had the unique blessing of Isaac:

> Cursed be everyone who curses you,
> And blessed be those who bless you
>
> Gen 27:29 (NKJV)

Flowing to the children of God is Jacob's unique blessing as well. It is endemic to the new birth. This enables the saint of God to walk among men with special power.

Moses, who is cited 850 times in Scripture, exercised his righteousness and holiness as a continual action before God.

> But since then there has not arisen in Israel a prophet like Moses, whom the LORD knew face to face, in all the signs and wonders which the LORD sent him to do in the land of Egypt, before Pharaoh, before all his servants, and in all his land, and by all that <u>mighty power and all the great terror</u> which Moses performed in the sight of all Israel.
>
> Deuteronomy 34:10-12 (NKJV)

178

(Few times, since the early church, has there been such a testimony before the world, but there must be now—in these last days—such a testimony again! God's children must be characterized by these two qualities: mighty power and a power that strikes terror in the heart of the unrighteous.)

Persons of faith follow in rapid order in this great chapter of Hebrews 11. Joshua and Rahab, alongside all those who were mentioned previously, became severally and individually a part of verse 33. Following the summary of spiritual giants: Gideon, Barak, Sampson, Jephthah, David and Samuel, (a Bible search of their righteous and holy lives is most rewarding), the author begins the exploit-summary which characterized the entire lot.

> ...who through faith subdued kingdoms,
> **worked righteousness**,...
>
> Hebrews 11:33 (NKJV)

Although the passage is much longer with mighty exploits, for the purpose of this study, the phrase, "worked righteousness" is worthy of scrutiny. All the exploits enumerated in the verses following this verse were done by people of faith who possessed righteousness. With righteousness working in them, they worked out, with fear and trembling, their own salvation! The hall of fame could not help incorporating them, for they all possessed one testimony: "The world was not worthy" of them.

Thousands upon the earth TODAY should have this testimony. The perfection of the kingdom will not be complete without righteous exploits working in modern hearts. The works of righteousness ARE the deeds of exploit! Righteous exploits once more must be seen on the earth. God's hall of fame is not closed till further notice; it is open for new entrants.

In hamlets, villages, towns, cities and mega-cities, there

are thousands whose hearts are yielded to God like those of the Old Testament. To them, "God has something better (Hebrews 11:40 NKJV)." (Not only has He given His Son, but He has given His Spirit.) Equipped with salvation and filling, there must rise a "generation of the chosen" who will again bring exploits to the earth. Just as faith moved those with lesser anointing into the hall of fame in Hebrews 11, there needs to be those of the Twenty-first Century, qualifying themselves for the latter day hall of fame. The cloud of witnesses who review this generation surely has not closed ranks, but how will they reckon with what they observe? A weak testimony will not bring them cheering to their feet, but exploits will.

No greater time in history can be found than this time. The world is in great flux, and opportunity has never been better than now to fulfill Psalms 2:8, "Ask of Me, and I will give you the nations."

The saints of God who have been mentioned throughout this book have been placed strategically by the Holy Spirit to encourage and strengthen those who are about to be emboldened in their faith. Every sentence, every Biblical study was used with one purpose in mind—to call for a degree of righteousness and holiness that has not coursed this earth since the days of the Apostles and Prophets. Nothing else will suffice, for if in the end time, the two witnesses lie dead in the streets, the greatest exposé of God-power since the resurrection of His Son is about to take place. Those two will rise—to the fear and consternation of the politico-religious forum gathered to cheer their demise.

> ...and the graves were opened; and many bodies of the saints who had fallen asleep were raised; and coming out of the graves after His resurrection, they went into the holy city and

180

appeared to many.
Matthew 27:52-53 (NKJV)

(The Lord did this once; He can do it again.)

Just when the world thought a celebration was in order, Righteousness and Holiness rise to call down judgment and do exploits. It is time for the saints to practice. It is time to prepare. The high calling may soon be heard and someone must be ready for the charge. Someone must step up and declare his or her standing as a saint! Someone must believe the scripture and embrace those "saint-things" that are given!

> As for the saints who are on the earth, "They are the excellent ones, in whom is all my delight."   Psalms 16:3 (NKJV)

> Oh, fear the LORD, you His saints! There is no want to those who fear Him.
> Psalms 34:9 (NKJV)

> Let the saints be joyful in glory;
> Let them sing aloud on their beds.
> Let the high praises of God be in their mouth,
> And a two-edged sword in their hand,
> To execute vengeance on the nations,
> And punishments on the peoples;
> To bind their kings with chains,
> And their nobles with fetters of iron;
> To execute on them the written judgment —
> **This honor have all His saints**.
> Praise the LORD!
> Psalms 149:5-9 (NKJV)

> But the saints of the Most High shall receive the kingdom, and possess the kingdom forever, even forever and ever.'
> Daniel 7:18-19 (NKJV)

I was watching; and the same horn was making war against the saints, and prevailing against them, **until** the Ancient of Days came, and a judgment was made in favor of the saints of the Most High, and the time came for the saints to possess the kingdom.

Daniel 7:21-22 (NKJV)

Now He who searches the hearts knows what the mind of the Spirit is, because He makes intercession for the saints according to the will of God. And we know that all things work together for good to those who love God, to those who are the called according to His purpose.

Romans 8:27-28 (NKJV)

(Verse 28 is quoted often, but it ONLY belongs to the saints who are called to His purpose)

Do you not know that the saints will judge the world? And if the world will be judged by you, are you unworthy to judge the smallest matters? Do you not know that we shall judge angels? How much more, things that pertain to this life? 1 Corinthians 6:2-3 (NKJV)

may be able to comprehend with all the saints what is the width and length and depth and height— to know the love of Christ which passes knowledge; that you may be filled with all the fullness of God. Now to Him who is able to do exceedingly abundantly above all that we ask or think, according to the power that works in us, to Him be glory in the church by Christ Jesus to all generations, forever and ever. Amen. Ephesians 3:18-21 (NKJV)

...giving thanks to the Father who has qualified us to be partakers of the inheritance of the saints in the light. He has delivered us from the power of darkness and conveyed us into the kingdom of the Son of His love

Colossians 1:12-13 (NKJV)

Beloved, while I was very diligent to write to you concerning our common salvation, I found it necessary to write to you exhorting you to contend earnestly for the faith which was once for all delivered to the saints. For certain men have crept in unnoticed...   Jude 3-4 (NKJV)

Now Enoch, the seventh from Adam, prophesied about these men also, saying, 'Behold, the Lord comes with ten thousands of His saints, **to execute judgment** on all, **to convict** all who are ungodly among them of all their ungodly deeds which they have committed in an ungodly way, and of all the harsh things which ungodly sinners have spoken against Him.'   Jude 14-15 (NKJV)

And the smoke of the incense, with the prayers of the saints, ascended before God from the angel's hand. Then the angel took the censer, filled it with fire from the altar, and threw it to the earth. And there were **noises, thunderings, lightnings**, and an **earthquake**.

Revelation 8:4-5 (NKJV)

(These are power prayers from saints of exploit)

And to her it was granted to be arrayed in fine linen, clean and bright, for the fine linen is the

righteous acts of the saints. Then he said to me, "Write: 'Blessed are those who are called to the marriage supper of the Lamb!"

Revelation 19:8-9 (NKJV)

These passages have been just a few which call for the "saints" to step forward and be counted. Too long, the church and the world have been misled as to who the saints are and what they are about. Let them be known as the "sanctified" ones, who exist sans church or prelate, for they possess His Righteousness and His Holiness—the inseparable twins of God!

The Crushing of the Holy People

Keil & Delitzsch, review this passage in Daniel 7 with a depth beyond the average Bible commentator. They show the context of the word and examine the powerful shattering of the Holy People of God in the end times. Scholarship must acknowledge the last days bring about unusual pressure on the saints. **This is the exact text of the commentary. It is the primary resource for this book's study on the subject.**

> Dan 12:4-13
> Judas Maccabaeus brought back their people
> to Judea who were living scattered among the
> heathen in Galilee and Gilead
> (1 Macc. 5:23, 45, 53, 54).

But against such an interpretation of the word napeets (OT:5310), Hofmann (Weiss. u. Erf. i. p. 314) has with justice replied, that the reference to the reunion of Israel, which is nowhere else presented in Daniel, would enter very unexpectedly into this connection, besides that napeets (OT:5310) does not agree with its object yaad (OT:3027), though we should translate this by "might," or altogether improperly by "part." yaad (OT:3027) has not the meaning "part," which is attributed to it only on the ground of an incorrect interpretation of certain passages. napeets (OT:5310) signifies to beat to pieces, to shatter; cf. Ps 2:9; 137:9, and in the Pu. Isa 27:9. This is the primary meaning of the word, from which is attempted to be derived the meaning, to burst asunder, to scatter. This primary meaning of the word, however, Hengstenberg, Maurer, Auberlen, Kranichfeld, Kliefoth, and Ewald have rightly maintained in this place.

Only we may not, with them, translate kalowt (OT:3615) by: to have an end, for then the answer would be tautological, since the breaking to pieces of the might of the people is identical with their scattering, but it has the meaning to make perfect, to accomplish, so that nothing more remains to be done. yaad (OT:3027), hand, is the emblem of active power; the shattering of the hand is thus the complete destruction of power to work, the placing in a helpless and powerless condition, such as Moses has described in the words yaad (OT:3027) 'aazalat (OT:235) kiy (OT:3588) (for the hand is gone), Deut 32:36, and announced that when this state of things shall arise, then "the Lord shall judge His people, and repent Himself for His servants." With this harmonizes the conclusion of the oath: then all these things shall be finished, or shall complete themselves. kaal-'eeleh (all these things) are the palaa'owt (OT:6382), v. 6.

To these "wonderful things" belong not merely the crushing of the holy people in the tribulation such as never was before, but also their deliverance by the coming of the angel-prince Michael, the resurrection of the dead, and the eternal separation of the righteous from the wicked (Dan 12:1-3). This last designation of the period of time goes thus, beyond a doubt, to the end of all things, or to the consummation of the kingdom of God by the resurrection of the dead and the final judgment. With this also agrees with expression qodesh (OT:6944) `am (OT:5971), which is not to be limited to the converted Jews. The circumstance that in Daniel's time the Israel according to the flesh constituted the "holy people," does not necessitate our understanding this people when the people of God are spoken of in the time of the end, since then the faithful from among all nations shall be the holy people of God.

(from Keil & Delitzsch Commentary on the Old Testament: New Updated Edition, Electronic Database. Copyright (c) 1996 by Hendrickson Publishers, Inc.)

Epilogue

During the writing of this text, various and sundry persons felt the leadership of the Spirit to call, email or write and give a prophesy, recommend a website, share their insights or point to a resource. Many of them were unaware they were being led of the Spirit to guide the author in a direction which would eventually be a turning point or the quintessence of illustration or support. Among them was Mr. Ed Minor and Col. Mac Kendrick. Also during the writing period, which covered nearly a year, invitations would arise to speak across the country. Naturally, most of what was shared related to the research, revelation or concerns of Holiness and Righteousness. Many of these churches and groups added honing to the subject matter and gave the author direct input, thus affording him opportunity for a "live test" of the material. Prominent among these was World Outreach Worship Center in Newport News, Va., first under the hand of Rev. J.R. Gurley, youth pastor, and on a second occasion under the leadership of the pastors Rev. Bob and Dot Collins and Rev. Russell and Sylvia Evenson. Other fellowships in the eastern

Virginia areas shared their support: Cindy Foster's Beauty for Ashes Ministry, New Smyrna Worship Center and Alton and Jackie Cagle Ministries. New Life Christian Center in Lead Hill, Ark., under the direction of Art and Leonard Miller, as well as the home fellowships of Joe and Lynn Price of Ft. Worth, shared their people, love and time while grasping the truths of this book.

Space will not allow for the naming of all those who were integral to the support and encouragement needed to complete the task. To those unnamed, please know your sharing and love will not be forgotten by the Heavenly Father or by me.

Dr. C.R. Oliver

Additional Works By Dr. C.R. Oliver

Solomon' Secret, now in its second edition, is a full commentary on the *Song of Solomon*. Utilizing the author's literary background and over twenty years of study,
combined with the revelation by the Spirit, the text emerges as a prophesy for the Last Days. In a simple verse by verse approach, the unity of the book is kept moving by its
dramatic form. Many readers have remarked, "I never viewed the Song in this manner before; this text has changed my thinking." As a guide to becoming Christ's Bride, *Solomon's Secret* eclipses those texts who merely think of the Song as a marriage source.
This book is used in various Bible schools across the world as a textbook during Old Testament survey.
US $12.95 Spanish and English Versions

Sons of Zadok, in its fourth printing, has been distributed worldwide and enjoys a continuing success. Focusing on the Zadok (Righteous) Priesthood, it condemns the
Eli system and elevates those who teach the difference between the holy and the profane.
Used as a standard text for many ministerial schools, it offers the reader a tool for appraising ministries across the board. Over 300 pages are dedicated to an intense Bible
study and is an affordable material for home fellowships and Bible study groups.
US$10.95 Spanish and English Versions

En Punto, in either the English or Spanish Versions, is a timely look at hitting the "mark" and accomplishing the will of God, rather than "missing the mark." For nearly 300 pages, it incorporates both Old and New Testament Bible study ranging from surveys of whole Books (Ezekiel, Acts) to indepth word study of related passages and themes. Staying the course, following the exact commands of Father and the Spirit and walking daily in the power of being in His will, are examined.

 US $14.95 Spanish (Fall 2003) and English Versions

The Regal Pair offers the reader a summary of every Biblical passage on the subject of Holiness and Righteousness. It divides the subject matter text along Hebrew and

Greek derivations for the noun and adjective form and offers clarity of dimension along the way. Such a large subject base, entangled often by theologians in doctrinal bias,

has proven the need for this study among Spirit-led believers. Its clear approach incorporates the works of Finney, Frelinghuysen, Spurgeon and Lake, summarizing their insights on H&R.

US $12.95 Spanish and English

Sealed Unto His Coming is a future text and fifth in the series of interrelated subjects. This book will bring full circle back to Solomon's writings and study what should be

Sealed and what is sealed unto the day of Christ's return. (No Publishing date)

View the official website: www.zadokpublications.com <http://www.zadokpublications.com/> /order direct from zadokbookstore@yahoo.com < mail to:zadokbookstore@yahoo.com> or email Dr. Oliver at zadok8@yahoo.com

About The Author

Dr. C.R. Oliver is a retired college professor and an ordained minister.

As professor, he taught a range of College subjects. Although credentialed in Behavioral Science, he also utilized His theological degrees by teaching Biblical Studies and Philosophy. He has published in Reflessi, the International Journal for Counseling; Church Administration, Family Life (Popenoe Institute) Southwestern Sociological Association Journal and the American Journal of Sociology. He has lectured both in the U.S. and abroad and chaired several organizations of behavioral science.

As Minister, he served twenty-eight years as pastor alongside teaching and other duties. Ministering in 53 countries, both in education and religion, his range of duties extended from establishing missions in third world countries to advising and assisting multiple missionary enterprises. His works reflect many of his experiences in these fields of service.

As Author, he is credited with four books, which are detailed in this volume, plus has been involved in several editing and advising capacities with other religious writers. Due to the popularity of his work, he has been privileged to maintain speaking tours both in the U.S. and abroad.

As President, of OEA International, a non-profit missionary organization, he has continued his involvement (even in retirement) with several worthwhile evangelistic and missionary endeavors. Africa, India and various areas of South America have benefited from the organization's generosity. Zadok Publications, the publishing arm of OEA, Int., has supplied thousands of dollars of English and Spanish texts to assist pastors and church leaders.

Visit the website: **www.oliverevangelisticassociation.org**

Bibliography

Chapter One:

(1) (Paraphrased account) Bright, Bill, "An Incredible story," email letter July, 24, 2002.

Chapter Two

(1) Lake, John G., John G. Lake His Life, His Sermons, His Boldness of Faith, Kenneth Copeland Publications, Ft. Worth, Texas, 1994, pages 401-2.

(2) Excerpts from Russell Stendal's promotion of the *Jubilee Bible*,2003.

Chapter Three:

(1) Holiness Essential to Salvation, Rev. C.G. Finney, Oberlin Collegiate Institute, Moorfield Tabernacle, England, 1850 (www.GospelTruth.net).

(2) Ibid

(3) Ibid

(4) Finney, Chas. "Charles G. Finney's Memoirs," Chapter XXVII, Fall 1843 to March, 1844 (Finney's Higher Life Experience in 1843). Received as email from edwardminer@hotmail.com 12/13/02

(5) Ibid

(6) Jamieson, Fausset, and Brown Commentary, Electronic Database, Biblesoft, 1997 (Comments on Daniel 12:7)

(7) Ibid

(8) A current theology, spearheaded by Bishop Carlton Pearson of Oklahoma, is that all the people of the earth are forgiven through the work of the cross automatically and that none will perish unless they overtly object.

Chapter Five

(1) Mitchell, A. (from a discussion at Hillsdale College, Hillsdale, Michigan) http://www.hillsdale.edu/dept/Phil&Rel/JE/Papers/ 98/ MitchellA.html

(2) Nee, Watchman, <http://www.appliedchrisstiantruths.org/ tp30046 2 5 0.htm>

Chapter Six

(1) Campbell, Wendy, *Why North West Arkansas?*, http://www.joyshoppe.com/conference/nwarkansas.htm

(2) For a study on portals, check these websites and titles: *Portals of Glory,* by Pat Cocking, http://www.the-war-room.com *Heavenly Portals*, by John Paul Jackson, http://www.streamsministries.com

The Elijah List, by Steve Shultz, <http://www.elijahlist.com/>

(3) Op. cit., Campbell, Wendy

Chapter Seven, Holy Is

1. Vine, W.E., *Vine's Expository Dictionary of Biblical Words*, Thomas Nelson Publishers, 1985

Chapter Eight: Something Is Missing in the Temple

1. Adam Clarke's Commentary, Electronic Database, Biblesoft, 1996

2. ibid

3. ibid

4. Matthew Henry's Commentary on the Whole Bible: New Modern Edition, Electronic Database. Copyright 1991 by Hendrickson Publishers, Inc.

5. ibid

Chapter Nine:

1. Spurgeon, Charles Haddon, Morning and Evening Lectures, Electronic Database, Biblesoft, 1996

2. Roos, Grace, Excerpt from *The Voice and Leading of God*, The Glory Watch (Magazine), Winter/Spring 2003, Branson, Mo., page 7

3. Spurgeon, Charles Haddon, *Morning and Evening Lectures*, Electronic Database, Biblesoft, 1996

4. Ibid

5. Lake, John G., *John G. Lake, His Life, His Sermons, His Boldness of Faith*, Kenneth Copeland Publications, Ft. Worth, Texas, 1994, page 344

Chapter 10 Righteous Determination

1. Great Awakening, The Columbia Encyclopedia, Sixth Edition, 2001, http://wwww.bartleby.com/65/gr/GreatAwa.html

2. Roberts, Richard Owen, *Salvation In Full Color*, International Awakening Ministries, Wheaton, Illinois

3. Ibid

4. Ibid

5. Ibid (excerpts from)

Chapter Eleven

1. Melbourne, Colin, *How to Obtain Perfect Righteousness*